PRINCE DUSTIN
AND
CLARA

PRINCE DUSTIN
AND
CLARA

DEEP IN THE BLACK FOREST

By

DANIEL LEE NICHOLSON

Fossil Mountain Publishing, LLC

FOSSIL
MOUNTAIN PUBLISHING

ACKNOWLEDGMENTS

Fossil Mountain Publishing would like to thank the dance, performing and fine arts communities for their commitment to providing excellence in instruction and their devotion to inspiring our youth. There is no limit to what a person can do that has been inspired by the arts!

Printed in the United States of America

First Edition / Hardcover

Library of Congress Control Number: 2017937239

ISBN-13: 978-0-9986191-1-8 (Hardcover)
ISBN-13: 978-0-9986191-0-1 (Paperback)
ISBN-13: 978-0-9986191-2-5 (ebook)

Fossil Mountain Publishing
PO BOX 48092
Watauga, TX 76148

www.FossilMountainPublishing.com

for Daisy

TABLE OF CONTENTS

PROLOGUE

ACT 1

ACT 2

ACT 3

❖ ❖ ❖

DEEP IN THE BLACK FOREST

BOOK ONE

Prologue

-PROLOGUE-

Christmas Eve

On a crisp Christmas Eve many, many years ago, snowflakes danced with the wind, while the moon glowed a bright orange hue, casting a rainbow of magnificent shades of purple across the night sky. Although early in the evening, the skies were cloaked in darkness. Against the black of the night, mounds of fresh snow appeared effervescent and glistened, inviting all for a sleigh ride beneath the twinkling stars. Elegant horse-drawn carriages, elaborately adorned, some with leather seats and gaudy gold detailing, lined the streets. The smell of fresh baked Bauernbrot and roasted chestnuts teased everyone within a mile of the bakery on the corner of Kunkel Street.

The animals even seemed to know this was a magical night unlike any other. The neighborhood dogs seemed to be playing tag with the ever-present alley cats. Any other night, the dogs would be chasing the cats up a nearby tree, barking at them from down below. Yes, tonight would be a special night of mystery, magic, and faraway places.

Of all the grand houses on all the streets, one house seemed, even more, special tonight. It had no more lights or wreaths of pine, not even more mounds of snow. Nobody understood or could fully explain it, but the magic of the night seemed to be coming from this particular house. It was the home of Dr. and Mrs. Stahlbaum, their daughter, Clara, and son, Fritz.

The brightest star in the sky even seemed to know something magical was about to happen. It seemed to be shining down directly on the Stahlbaums' home. The star hit the top of the pitched red clay roof and gables, totally illuminating the mansion, like a Christmas tree adorned with glimmering candle lights on every branch. The house seemed to be personally inviting all that passed to rip and romp, frolic and play. Tonight, the Stahlbaums would host their annual Christmas Eve party, and the magic had already begun.

Everyone who walked by the Stahlbaums' home got a funny, tickling sensation in the pit of their stomach. Adults, feeling slightly unsettled, sneaked a peek behind them for the cause of the funny feeling. Smaller kids, full of glee, giggled and laughed while holding their stomachs. It felt like their bellies were doing somersaults. The children hopped back and forth, then forth and back, as if each wanted another ride.

DEEP IN THE BLACK FOREST

Nobody seemed to notice the strange-looking chap dressed all in black watching everyone from the side of the house. Those who did might have thought, from his wide smile and laughter, that although mysterious-looking with his rumpled top hat and swinging black cape, he was harmless enough. *Just another frolicker enjoying the evening*, they thought.

"Every hour of every day, poor Helmut had to endure the cuckoos."

ACT 1

·1·

Clara and Fritz

"Fritz!"

Fritz was panting. He heard his mother screaming but kept running. He thought he could delay the agony a little longer, so he bolted up the staircase and down the long hallway.

"Fritz! I know you hear me!"

"He does this every year," Mrs. Koch, the head cook, said with a frustrated tone.

Mrs. Stahlbaum replied, "I told Dr. Stahlbaum to have a talk with him."

"And that wasn't the worst of it. He scared poor Amalie out of her wits," Mrs. Koch continued. "And trust me it doesn't take much to scare that poor girl."

❖ ❖ ❖

What did Fritz do now? Clara was in her bedroom. She was getting dressed for her parents' annual

Christmas Eve party when she heard her mother yelling after Fritz. He was always getting into trouble.

Clara thought back to the previous week when Fritz had played a trick on the young maid, Amalie. He kept ringing the doorbell while Amalie was cooking. Each time Amalie made it to the front door, nobody was on the other side. He did this several times before the young maid caught on.

Mrs. Stahlbaum told Clara's father, Dr. Stahlbaum, to have a talk with Fritz about playing tricks on the house staff. However, Dr. Stahlbaum ended up laughing hysterically after hearing Fritz describe the look on the young maid's face. Fritz had a way of making everything sound funny.

The smell of smoky katenspek savory ham with cinnamon and brown sugar filled the air. "Mmmm!" Clara cooed as she took a whiff. She could hardly wait for the party to start. Each year, it would be the talk of the town for several weeks. All of Clara's friends and their parents were expected to come.

Looking into the mirror on her bureau, Clara pulled at the spiral-shaped curls of her long, thick, chestnut brown hair. Her eyes were the same color and were highlighted by long eyelashes. All her life people told her that she had big, beautiful brown eyes. She blinked, wondering if she was old enough to wear make-up.

Clara barely slept the night before. All she could think about was dancing and having fun with her friends. She and her friends took dance from the same dance teacher, Miss Patti. Miss Patti often chose Clara to demonstrate to the class.

"Hahahahaha!"

Giddy laughter was coming from outside. Clara glanced out of her bedroom window. It had stopped snowing earlier in the day. The fresh snow was pure white, sparkling almost like the snow was mixed with diamonds. From her window, Clara saw several people she knew. They were all dressed up. Clara thought it strange that a crowd had formed in front of her house.

Clara saw Mrs. Brecht and her three boys. Clara didn't like Mrs. Brecht's sons. *I'm glad they weren't invited.* Clara still remembered what they had done, earlier in the year, at her twelfth birthday party. When her mother and all the other ladies went into the side parlor, the Brecht boys, along with Fritz, chased and teased all the girls. Sarah's little sister started crying. Everyone ended up leaving the party early. *It was the worst party ever*, Clara sighed remembering.

Clara looked closer at the Brecht boys. *Those silly boys.* Even for them, they were acting oddly, Clara thought. They were running back and forth in front of her house, laughing raucously and waving their arms wildly in the air. The youngest one was smiling and holding his belly. Clara squinted for a sharper look.

Clara fleetingly thought about grabbing a handful of snow and forming a ball to aim straight at them. She didn't though. Deep down, she was too afraid to do anything that could get her in trouble. Clara secretly wished she had the courage to be more daring like her brother Fritz.

"Fritz!" Mrs. Stahlbaum screamed, even louder than before. Hearing her mother, Clara dashed out of her bedroom to see what Fritz had done. She nearly collided into him. Fritz scuttled past Clara and darted straight into her bedroom. Clara followed angrily.

"Mother is calling you. Didn't you hear her?"

Fritz looked up at Clara with *that same innocent look* he had every time he got into trouble. It worked most times. Although Mrs. Stahlbaum got frustrated with some of Fritz's antics, she could barely get too upset with him. Dr. Stahlbaum found Fritz's actions amusing. Each time he would have a stern talk with Fritz and Fritz would be good for a day or so. However, Fritz just couldn't help himself and would soon find himself in some other trouble.

Even Clara couldn't get too mad at Fritz. When he was a baby, Clara played with him like he was a doll. He was more fun to play with than any of her actual dolls. Mrs. Stahlbaum let Clara take him for strolls in her doll carriage and feed him his bottle. Clara and Fritz were actually very close. But like most young boys, the people they like the most, they taunted the most, for Fritz, that was Clara.

When Fritz was a toddler, people thought he was a girl. He had big brown eyes, long eyelashes, and thick, dark chestnut-colored hair, just like Clara. His hair always looked tousled. Mrs. Stahlbaum's friends still oohed and ahhed over Fritz, so he avoided them. Even though he used his baby face to get out of trouble, he didn't like Mrs. Stahlbaum's friends treating him like he *was* a baby.

Fritz looked up at Clara with a mouthful of gingerbread cookies. Crumbs had fallen down to his chin. Clara stared back at Fritz's innocent look and thought it wasn't going to help him this time. They heard footsteps coming down the hallway.

CLICK CLICK CLICK CLICK CLICK CLICK!

Clara pointed toward the hallway as she looked at Fritz, "Mom is looking for you!"

Fritz gulped as he took the remaining gingerbread cookies he was holding and quickly stuffed them into his pants pocket. Clara didn't seem to notice a creepy thick white rubber-looking string dangling back and forth from the breast pocket of Fritz's shirt. Nor did she seem to notice Fritz gently tuck it down deeper into his pocket.

"Fritz Baldric Stahlbaum, didn't you hear me calling you?" Mrs. Stahlbaum said sharply, using Fritz's full name as she entered Clara's bedroom.

"No, I didn't hear you, Mom. Did you call me?" Fritz replied innocently, with *that* look.

Mrs. Stahlbaum regarded Fritz with a look of disbelief, "Haven't we told you often enough not to take your mouse out of its cage?"

Fritz avoided eye contact with his mother. He looked down at the floor and brushed his foot from side to side as if wondering what he could say to get out of this one.

"Mrs. Koch said Amalie had just set out the platter of gingerbread cookies when you snuck right behind Amalie and grabbed a handful," Mrs. Stahlbaum said angrily.

Fritz continued looking down.

"When she came back to set out the dessert plates and napkins, she caught you."

Fritz, still looking down, twisted his lip in silence.

"And when she told you to stop grabbing the cookies, you took your mouse out of your pocket and held it up to her and asked her if she wanted to pet it!" Mrs. Stahlbaum's voice was getting louder and louder as she recounted the story.

Clara opened her eyes and mouth widely after hearing what Fritz had done.

Fritz swallowed. A line of saliva could be seen inching down his throat.

"Did you really do that, Fritz?" Mrs. Stahlbaum asked.

Fritz didn't respond. He looked up at his mom with *that innocent look.* He then opened his mouth to speak, but Mrs. Stahlbaum cut him off sharply.

"If you let that mouse out one more time, I'm going to have Mr. Godfrey be done with it. Do you understand me, Fritz?"

Still looking down, Fritz replied softly, "Yes, Mom." His eyes moved in unison from side to side.

Mrs. Stahlbaum shook her head as she left Clara's bedroom.

Clara looked at Fritz. Her cheeks were red and puffy. "You better be glad I didn't tell Mom that you put the gingerbread cookies in your *dress* pants."

"Uh, thanks."

Clara walked toward her closet. She had succumbed to *that innocent look.* She reasoned it was just a matter of time before Fritz would get into trouble again anyway. Clara thought about how bold he was, Fritz was never afraid.

Clara, however, was afraid of all sorts of things. She was afraid of getting into trouble, so she always did what her parents told her to do. She was afraid of disappointing her teachers, so she studied extra hard to get high marks in her classes. She was afraid of sudden shadows and jumped if someone came up from behind. She was also afraid of doing and trying anything different, so she resisted requests from her friends to try new things. But more than anything else, Clara was afraid of animals. Even small animals had sharp teeth and claws, Clara acknowledged.

Every spring Dr. and Mrs. Stahlbaum would take Clara and Fritz on a trip to visit Herr Drosselmeyer in the Black Forest. Although Clara and Fritz called him uncle, Herr Drosselmeyer was actually of no relation, just a close family friend. Clara always looked forward to the trips. Nervously she would keep an eye out for small animals, often jumping at every sound.

She loved hearing about the legends of the Black Forest. Clara wanted to believe the legends were true. *Deep in the Black Forest*, legend had it that kingdoms with brave kings and princes and beautiful queens and princesses were plentiful. However, it was also part of the folklore that all kinds of strange and scary things happened deep in the Black Forest. Although the stories spooked Clara, she was still captivated by the tales.

❖ ❖ ❖

Fritz enjoyed the visits to the Black Forest as much as Clara. Last spring, after the last of the snow melted from the mountaintops, the Stahlbaums went to visit Herr Drosselmeyer.

While traveling through the Black Forest, they stopped at one of the small villages. Many craftsmen lived there. The craftsmen had shops where they made all kinds of things. In one of the shops, the shopkeeper was an expert craftsman of small wind-up metal toys.

Toy soldiers, animals, and dolls, made of tin, were all around his shop. Fritz immediately spotted a rather large tin toy soldier on one of the top shelves. It was much larger than anything else in the shop. It was colorfully painted. The toy soldier's uniform was bright red and blue.

Fritz wondered what it did when it was wound up. He *had* to get a closer view. He glanced over at his dad. Dr. Stahlbaum and the shopkeeper were engaged in conversation. Fritz then scanned the front of the shop. Mrs. Stahlbaum and Clara were out of view, hidden behind tall shelving units. Fritz heard his mom and Clara chattering cheerfully. They sounded delighted and were busy with what they had found. *Probably a wind-up doll*, Fritz thought.

"Sure, we get orders from all around the world for our toys," Fritz heard the shopkeeper respond to his dad. Fritz then looked up curiously at the large tin toy soldier. He couldn't resist.

Fritz smiled. *Nobody would see me*, he figured. He wondered if the tin soldier wielded its sword when it was completely wound up. Or maybe it would march in precise fashion like a real soldier. He wasn't sure what it did, *but he had to know.*

Fritz looked around the shop. He saw a counter stool in the back corner. He rolled it over to the shelving unit. Fritz heard his mom and Clara. They were still in the front of the store. He looked around and saw his father and the shopkeeper. They were still talking and laughing.

Fritz steadily climbed up on the counter stool. He held onto one of the shelves for balance so the stool wouldn't wobble or roll. Stepping high on his toes, Fritz reached up to grab the toy soldier. He was unable to reach it. He took another look around the room before stepping off the seat of the stool and onto one of the higher shelves. He smiled as he grabbed the large tin toy soldier.

Then—*it happened*!

CLINK CLINK PLOP PLOP CLINK CLINK PLOP PLOP CLINK CLINK PLOP PLOP!

Fritz slipped off the shelving unit! All the toys fell and crashed on the floor around him. His fall was cushioned by a large pillow the shopkeeper kept on the floor near the shelving unit for his dog

The shopkeeper must have seen Fritz. Right before *it happened*, he ran over to the shelving unit and caught it from falling down on Fritz.

Hearing the loud clattering sound, Clara, Dr. and Mrs. Stahlbaum all ran over and looked down at Fritz.

Fritz looked at all the toys around him. He spotted the large tin toy soldier. It had fallen right next to him. Fritz lifted his hand and was about to grab it when he saw his dad's boots. The boots seemed even bigger at eye level. Fritz thought frantically as he pulled his hand back. He dared not grab the tin toy soldier now.

How did that happen, Fritz lamented. He then looked up at everyone with *that innocent look.*

The Stahlbaums ended their trip with a visit to Herr Drosselmeyer's old mill. Clara and Fritz were always so excited to see the new toys their Uncle Drosselmeyer made. Everyone knew Herr Drosselmeyer was the best toymaker in all of the Black Forest. People from the village were in awe of his toys. They seemed magical and hypnotizing, almost real. *Not like toys at all.*

After the incident at the toy store, Dr. Stahlbaum kept a close eye on Fritz for the rest of the trip.

❖ ❖ ❖

CLICK CLICK CLICK CLICK CLICK CLICK!

Mrs. Stahlbaum was done scolding Fritz about the gingerbread cookies and could be heard walking briskly down the hallway. Fritz turned and glanced around. He was about to leave Clara's bedroom too. He then stopped and rubbed his chin. With a sly look, Fritz stared at Clara's dance slippers.

Clara was too busy getting ready for the party and didn't see Fritz staring at her slippers. She had set them on the floor next to her dresser bureau.

While moving slowly toward the slippers, Fritz asked Clara, "What do you think Uncle Drosselmeyer is going to give you for Christmas?"

Clara quickly turned around.

Fritz stopped in his tracks with his eyes wide open, when he saw Clara turn around.

"I don't know. I can't wait!" Clara responded. She then turned and reached back into her closet to grab something off the floor. Her box of ribbons and bows had fallen off the top shelf.

Fritz kept a steady eye on Clara this time as he inched closer to Clara's bureau.

Clara was now humming a Christmas song. Fritz smiled.

Silent night, holy night, all is calm, Clara hummed.

Fritz reached into the breast pocket of his shirt and pulled something out.

Holy infant so tender and mild, Clara continued humming, not noticing Fritz.

Fritz bent down and tucked something into Clara's dance slipper.

Clara continued humming, *Sleep in heavenly pe-eace.*

Fritz stood up and darted toward Clara's bedroom door. Before leaving her room, he stopped and innocently looked back at Clara, "I have to go finish getting dressed for the party."

❖ ❖ ❖

Clara walked toward her dresser bureau as Fritz left her bedroom. She heard his footsteps as he bolted down the hallway. Clara smiled thinking about Fritz. *He really isn't all that bad of a little brother,* she thought.

Clara slipped her foot into one of her dance slippers. She felt something furry inside. She then bent down to remove it. *Black pebble eyes* looked up at Clara.

"Aaaaaaaaaaaaaaaaaaaaaaaaaaaaaaagh!" Clara screamed.

SQUEAK SQUEAK SQUEAK SQUEAK SQUEAK SQUEAK SQUEAK SQUEAK!

Fritz's little white mouse squeaked as it jumped out of Clara's slipper and ran down the hall following Fritz.

-2-

Herr Drosselmeyer

"I've heard strange sounds coming from the mill in the middle of the night," said Mr. Greenberg with a curious look.

"They say that if you go there, you don't come back the same!" Mr. Hase exclaimed with a look of dread, shaking his head with fear.

❖ ❖ ❖

It was a couple of weeks before Christmas. Pine trees flocked by snow continued beyond what the eye could see. If it weren't for the accumulation of sharp icicles, hanging dangerously from the mountainside, it would look like a land of cotton candy. Although it was morning, half past eleven, all was dark in the Black Forest. The denseness of the trees didn't allow the sun to find a breach.

In an old mill at the edge of a lake, a flicker of light from the lower level indicated Herr Drosselmeyer was at work. He was a strange fellow, as much a part of the Black Forest as the trees. The children of the families who lived in the cottages in the Black Forest were both frightened and enchanted by him. The only thing the cottage people knew was that he was a toymaker.

He never seemed to get any older. The elders said that they were young when Drosselmeyer was old. Although they had now aged, many almost a century, Drosselmeyer remained the same. The elder men remembered being told stories about Herr Drosselmeyer when they were lads. Now they were the ones re-telling the tales.

Wearing black from head to toe, Drosselmeyer was an ominous sight to see. It was assumed he didn't have a change of clothes because he was always seen in the same black attire. Adding to his creepy presence was the black patch he wore covering his left eye. Legend had it he'd lost his eye while engaged in battle, fighting a giant mouse of human proportions. Whenever the cottage people were out and about and happened upon him, a chill went down their spines. They instinctively jumped.

To ease their discomfort, Drosselmeyer always extended to the cottage people courtesies usually only bestowed to those of a higher class. With great flair, he would grab the tail end of his long black cape in one hand. He would hold his flattened top hat in the other, acknowledging all he passed with a gentleman's bow and nod. No matter the time of day, Drosselmeyer always said, "Good day."

♦ ♦ ♦

Inside Drosselmeyer's old mill cuckoo clocks covered the walls of his parlor. Barely a speck of wall could be seen. Hundreds upon hundreds of cuckoo clocks were hung of all shapes and sizes. It was high noon. The walls seemed to come to life!

From all directions, the doors on all the clocks opened. The hidden cuckoo birds spun out and chirped loudly, "CUCKOO...CUCKOO...CUCKOO!"

CUCKOO   CUCKOO   CUCKOO   CUCKOO   CUCKOO CUCKOO CUCKOO!

CUCKOO   CUCKOO   CUCKOO   CUCKOO   CUCKOO CUCKOO CUCKOO!

CUCKOO   CUCKOO   CUCKOO   CUCKOO   CUCKOO CUCKOO CUCKOO!

The sound was deafening. Trying to escape the cackling cuckoos, Herr Drosselmeyer's dog, Helmut, dove underneath the dining table in the parlor and covered his ears with his front paws. However, there was no escape.

CUCKOO   CUCKOO   CUCKOO   CUCKOO   CUCKOO CUCKOO CUCKOO!

CUCKOO   CUCKOO   CUCKOO   CUCKOO   CUCKOO CUCKOO CUCKOO!

CUCKOO   CUCKOO   CUCKOO   CUCKOO   CUCKOO CUCKOO CUCKOO!

Although Helmut, a male Affenpinscher, a breed known to be ratters, was a very brave dog, he was no match against the spinning and chirping cuckoos. A minute later, all was silent. Helmut's ears drooped in relief. He had fifty-nine minutes of solitude before the cuckoos were released again. Every hour of every day, poor Helmut had to endure the cuckoos.

Helmut heard a continuous fast clicking sound. It would start then stop. Start then stop. Helmut jumped up and bolted toward the sound, wagging his tail eagerly.

In the kitchen, he slowed down momentarily and sniffed. Grilled bratwurst on a bed of sweet onions was on the counter. It was lunchtime. Although hungry, Helmut didn't linger. He continued down the back staircase. Muted light peeked through the kitchen window. The areas around the lakes and rivers of the Black Forest were the only places free of the continuous canopy of spruce and pine trees. The sun was bright in these areas. Every place else, nighttime seemed perpetual.

In the light that filtered through the kitchen window, Helmut's face looked human-like. His fur was jet-black and silky. His deep-set, onyx eyes and turned-up nose seemed to have a story to tell, possibly many stories. Helmut, always by the side of Herr Drosselmeyer, had seen much in his lifetime. Like Drosselmeyer, the dog showed no signs of aging. To the cottage people, that was also a mystery. Some would debate that it was a different dog than the one their grandfathers talked about in their folk tales. Others believed that whatever was keeping Drosselmeyer from aging was also keeping the dog from growing old.

DEEP IN THE BLACK FOREST

Helmut descended down the back stairs, moving more jauntily as he approached the bottom steps. The weight of his body pushed him down the stairs faster than his legs could actually go.

❖ ❖ ❖

Part of the folklore of the Black Forest was that Helmut was once a proud prince from a land deep in the Black Forest. As the legend went, one day, as often occurred in many of the kingdoms deep in the Black Forest, his kingdom was under attack. Prince Helmut led the charge and fought off the attackers, but he took a fatal stab to the chest. All thought Prince Helmut was dead. The people of his kingdom grieved for several days and nights.

A massive funeral was held for their beloved prince. Prince Helmut's body was lying on top of a raft decorated with violets and orchids. The raft was carried by the highest-ranking members of his army toward the river. A funeral procession, including all the people of Prince Helmut's kingdom, followed. Everyone walked in line to the edge of the river.

Prince Helmut's body was to be set ablaze by flaming arrows shot by his kingdom's best marksmen after the raft was downstream. Prince Helmut's spirit would then be released to continue in the afterlife. The afterlife was thought to be a land of beautiful, sunny countryside and endless happiness for all those allowed to enter. *The chosen ones.*

The raft was set on tree stumps placed at the river's bank so all could view Prince Helmut's body for a final farewell. Just before the raft was launched into the river, a strange old man appeared. He was dressed from head to toe in black, with a swinging black cape and rumpled top hat. He wore a black patch that covered his left eye.

Nobody had ever seen him before. All of the people from Prince Helmut's kingdom whispered comments about the strange man. Prince Helmut's army initially stood on alert. After a short time, they became entranced. They stood motionless. Something prevented them from moving.

The old man untied his cape and draped it over Prince Helmut's body. His cape covered Prince Helmut's body entirely. The old man then chanted words in a language nobody seemed to understand. All of the people of the kingdom watched and listened without saying a word.

The old man then knelt down and retrieved his cape. Everyone looked anxiously at the raft. The women shrieked and held their children closer. The men of the kingdom gripped their swords and weapons, not knowing what to expect. The army still stood motionless. All eyes were on the raft.

The raft was there, but Prince Helmut's body was gone! VANISHED! The violets and orchids that had lain on top of the body were now lying gently on the bed of the raft.

In the middle of the flowers was a small black dog. The dog's fur was jet-black and silky. It had deep-set eyes, the color of onyx, and a turned-up nose. The dog looked at the old man dressed in black and barked a friendly bark. The dog then jumped off the raft and wagged its tail while jumping up and down in front of the stranger. Everyone from Prince Helmut's kingdom watched in total silence. The stranger smiled and said something to the little black dog. Again, nobody seemed to understand.

All remained silent as the strange old man and the small black dog walked toward the wooded area of the forest. Once they reached the tall pine trees that led deeper into the Black Forest, they stopped. The dog turned around and held his head high. Very nobly, it barked a final farewell. After a few more steps into the woods, they were gone. Prince Helmut's body, the strange old man, and the small black dog were never seen again by the people of Prince Helmut's kingdom.

❖ ❖ ❖

Helmut reached the bottom of the staircase. He was now in the cellar of the old mill. The clicking sound was much louder. It was coming from the next room.

CLICK CLICK CLICK!

CLICK CLICK CLICK!

CLICK CLICK CLICK!

Helmut made it to the room with the clicking sound. It was dimly lit by flickering light coming from oil lamps. The room was dark and musty. It smelled like wet weeds.

Helmut moved toward a tall figure. A man stood in the middle of the room. Helmut wagged his tail the closer he got to the man. He stopped and sat directly in front of the man. The dog's tail was still wagging, gently brushing the floor.

Any person catching a glance would have been alarmed by the look of the man. He was dressed in black from head to toe. His movements were slow, as he bent down to rub Helmut on the back of his neck. The old man wore a patch that covered his left eye. His hair was gray and somewhat long for an old man, reaching the top of his shoulders. His facial features were sharp. He had a long and slender nose and gaunt cheeks. The iris of the eye not covered by the black patch was a very pale blue, almost white, ghastly white.

"Helmut," said Drosselmeyer, smiling as he continued to look down at the dog.

Helmut stopped wagging his tail and stood at attention.

Drosselmeyer acknowledged the dog and said, "At ease, Helmut." The dog then barked and sat on the left side of Drosselmeyer.

Two life-like figures, shorter than Drosselmeyer, were also in the center of the room. One was completely slumped over. The flickering light from the oil lamps cast an eerie and sinister-looking shadow against the cellar walls, giving movement to the still figures. Drosselmeyer reached behind the slumped-over figure and began turning what looked like a large key at the base of the back of the figure. The clicking sound resumed.

CLICK CLICK CLICK!
CLICK CLICK CLICK!
CLICK CLICK CLICK!

The slumped-over figure started moving. It moved slowly at first. It raised its head, then its shoulders. With its subtle movements, the figure looked like a person.

"Look, Helmut," Drosselmeyer said, stepping back to get a better view. "She is quite beautiful if I must say." Helmut cocked his head quizzically.

It was a girl, but not. She had a beautiful, chiseled, porcelain face with bright red cheeks. Her oval-shaped eyes were a deep, almost penetrating, emerald green. Her auburn hair was pulled back into loose curls. Her round chin was accented with a small dimple.

A green Juliet hat sat on the top of her head. It was slanted toward her face. The hat was heavily embellished with beads and a fan of tulle of the same color. It had green and black feathers on the side. Her dress, the same shade of green, flared out to a full skirt. Layers of white ruffles underneath her dress bounced as she moved.

"She is my best yet!" Drosselmeyer exclaimed, glaring at the girl that wasn't.

Helmut lied down flat on the cold concrete floor as he watched the doll come to life, as if unimpressed.

"Helmut, I am almost done with both these dolls for Clara," Drosselmeyer declared. Helmut raised his ears slightly, as though he cared. "They will entertain the guests at the Stahlbaums' Christmas party."

Helmut barked twice. Drosselmeyer smiled.

The beautiful Columbine doll began to dance. She extended her graceful arms above her head as she stepped gently forward. Standing on her toes, the doll spun around in a circle of pirouettes across the floor. The shadows cast against the wall were playful and lively, no longer eerie and sinister. After a few moments, the beautiful doll suddenly stopped. She was standing back where she started, right next to the other doll.

"I have to adjust her gears," muttered Drosselmeyer, placing his hands on his hips in frustration.

Helmut let out a soft bark while glancing up at the other figure. It was a young male doll. It stood erect with red cheeks similar to the beautiful girl doll. That, however, was where the resemblance ended. This doll was funny-looking, like a clown or joker. It was a Harlequin doll.

The legs of its pants were different colors: one red, the other gold. It wore a long-sleeved fitted top with red, black, and gold diamond shapes in a checkered design. The shirt was topped with an oversized ruffled collar extending past the Harlequin's shoulders.

"Look at the glint of his eyes, Helmut. His eyes almost look real. And his smile, he looks like he is laughing. My brew may have been a bit too strong when I built him," Drosselmeyer laughed haughtily, gazing at the Harlequin from head to toe.

The Harlequin's hat and shoes were most peculiar. The shoes curled up at the toes, anyone looking at the shoes would wonder if the doll's toes curled up, too. His hat sat low on his forehead. It was topped with three floppy ear-like extensions in red, green, and gold. Each extension had a pom-pom that flopped on the end. Helmut growled at the Harlequin doll.

Drosselmeyer responded, "You don't like the Harlequin doll? I guess the clothes do look a tad bit bizarre."

Helmut then growled a continuous low gruff at the Harlequin this time, gritting his teeth.

"Let's go upstairs, Helmut. I'll finish them later."

Drosselmeyer snuffed out the flames of the oil lamps, cupping his hand at the back of the lamps' chimneys and blowing out the flame, one lamp at a time. The room became increasingly darker with each flame he extinguished. Helmut followed behind. When Drosselmeyer got to the last lamp, he picked it up by its handle and walked out of the room. The room went completely black.

-3-

Christmas Eve Party

"Mr. Baumgartner must have had a hard time chopping this one down," said Mr. Godfrey, with a deep voice. He was the Stahlbaums' head of staff and butler.

Dr. Stahlbaum nodded as he looked up at the tall Christmas tree.

Overhearing the conversation as she stepped into the Stahlbaums' parlor, Mrs. Koch added, "I had to have Mr. Fenstermacher send over his tallest ladder, and Bernhard almost fell twice trying to put the ornaments on it."

Dr. Stahlbaum laughed. "I do believe this is the tallest tree we've ever had. Mrs. Stahlbaum will be delighted. She didn't think we had enough ornaments for the tree when it was delivered."

Mrs. Stahlbaum and the house staff prepared for weeks for the Stahlbaums' annual Christmas Eve party. Mrs. Stahlbaum had the house decorated lavishly with garland, red velvet ribbons, and wreaths made by an old lady who lived in a cottage in the Black Forest.

The grand staircase in the entrance foyer was loosely wrapped in spruce with red berries. Dishes filled with candy canes and platters of gingerbread cookies and pfeffernusse were placed on the center table in the foyer. The platters always held more pfeffernusse than gingerbread because Fritz always raided the gingerbread cookies before the party.

The entrance foyer led directly into the Stahlbaums' grand parlor. The parlor could accommodate dancing for groups of fifty people and maybe slightly more. The grand parlor had floor to ceiling windows with elaborate ornamental wood moldings. The windows were draped in heavy gold velvet and were always open to the street, except on very cold days. A roaring fire in the huge stone fireplace kept the parlor warm and cozy. A small balcony overlooking the entire room was used whenever the Stahlbaums entertained.

The Stahlbaums' Christmas tree was the main attraction. It was every bit of thirty feet tall, with ornaments the Stahlbaums had collected over the years. Some passed down through generations. The fresh scent of evergreen permeated through each room of the Stahlbaums' mansion. The fresh pine fragrance could even be smelled in the staff quarters, high above in the attic. The staff looked forward to Christmas as much as the Stahlbaums.

DEEP IN THE BLACK FOREST

A great-grandfather clock stood just inside the grand parlor. The pendulum inside its tower swung rhythmically back and forth. It was almost six o'clock in the evening, and all the servants were busy with the final details in preparation for the party.

Mrs. Stahlbaum joined Dr. Stahlbaum and the others in the grand parlor. She smiled as she looked up at the tall Christmas tree. "It looks like it could be standing in the middle of the Black Forest." She continued, "Except for the ornaments, of course."

Dr. Stahlbaum stood tall and gazed at Mrs. Stahlbaum. She was wearing a beautiful royal blue ball gown. Her hair was pinned high in an elaborate bun with tendrils of curls delicately framing her face. Mrs. Stahlbaum turned toward Dr. Stahlbaum and gave him a gentle kiss. Dr. Stahlbaum thought back to when he had first met Katharina.

❖ ❖ ❖

Dr. and Mrs. Stahlbaum met many years ago when they were both young adults. Dr. Stahlbaum was always well-liked by his friends and family. As a teenager, Wilhelm, or Will as his friends called him, was handsome, charismatic, and smart. Many of the girls wanted to date him, while the boys liked to challenge him in a game of cribbage. Will was an expert cribbage player and seldom lost, so he was admired, but often envied, by the boys. Although quite popular and well-regarded, Will was not arrogant at all.

He was an only child. His mother studied and taught classical dance and music. His father was a prominent doctor in town. When Will entered college, he followed in the footsteps of the Stahlbaum men for several generations by studying medicine.

In the last year of his medical studies, during winter break, Will's father and mother were hosting their annual Christmas dinner party. It was a smaller affair than the big galas he and Mrs. Stahlbaum currently held. Will was not looking forward to the party. His cousin Gretchen had invited one of her friends to the party. Will was expected to entertain them.

Gretchen and Will had always been close and although he enjoyed Gretchen's company, he would have preferred to camp out alone in his bedroom. He decided he would greet his cousin and her friend when they arrived and then politely excuse himself and sneak back up to his bedroom.

Gretchen and her friend arrived at the party early. Will was on the other side of the parlor. His cousin, Gretchen tapped him on his shoulder. "Will?"

Will turned and looked at his cousin. He then saw *her*.

When Gretchen introduced Katharina to Will, he was only able to mutter a barely distinguishable, "How da–uh how do–uh."

Gretchen mockingly said, "How do you do?"

A year later, Will and Katharina married.

❖ ❖ ❖

Mrs. Koch responded to Mrs. Stahlbaum's comment about the tall Christmas tree. "Yes, Mr. Baumgartner said he cut this one down from the river's edge, not too far from Herr Drosselmeyer's old mill."

With an inquisitive look, Dr. Stahlbaum wondered, "I can't wait to see what Herr Drosselmeyer has in store for us this year! He always delights all of the guests."

Mrs. Stahlbaum added, "Clara and Fritz have been talking all week about the surprises he will have for them this year. He always gives them great gifts."

Turning to Godfrey, Dr. Stahlbaum said, "Speaking of gifts, Godfrey, did you put all of the gifts under the tree for our guests? I had placed a few last-minute items on the table in the foyer."

Godfrey nodded. "Yes, Dr. Stahlbaum. I did retrieve those from the foyer and put them underneath the tree."

"Thank you," Dr. Stahlbaum replied.

Mrs. Stahlbaum said, "I'm going to check on dinner." She walked out of the grand parlor into the entrance foyer, followed by Mrs. Koch.

❖ ❖ ❖

"You have done an excellent job, as usual," Mrs. Stahlbaum said to Mrs. Koch. "Our guests are really going to enjoy your ham. I can smell it all the way from the kitchen. Did you prepare it differently this year?"

Mrs. Koch looked down as if embarrassed at the compliment, "Yes, I added extra brown sugar, peaches, and cinnamon to the glaze."

Mrs. Stahlbaum smiled delightedly. "Are the hors d'oeuvres ready? Our guests should be arriving shortly."

Before Mrs. Koch could respond, they heard Fritz and Clara coming down the grand staircase. Mrs.

Stahlbaum looked up to see Fritz galloping down the stairs with a look of anticipation that kids have when they wake on Christmas morning. He had put on a short, plum-colored velvet jacket that matched his lederhosen dress pants and wool stockings.

"You look quite handsome, Fritz," she said to him and then gave him a big hug.

Clara walked slowly down the grand staircase behind Fritz. She was dressed in a beautiful emerald green, shiny silk party dress. The petticoat was trimmed in white bows with several layers of ruffles. White fancy pantaloons, matching her petticoat, were worn underneath.

Hearing the children coming down the stairs, Dr. Stahlbaum stepped into the foyer. He looked up at Clara. "You look beautiful, Clara," he said. Clara smiled.

DING-DONG DING-DONG DING-DONG!

The first guests of the Stahlbaums' annual Christmas Eve party had arrived. Amalie with her holiday apron headed for the door.

Mrs. Stahlbaum took Fritz and Clara by their hands and gracefully escorted them into the grand parlor. Dr. Stahlbaum followed behind. He smiled as he looked at Mrs. Stahlbaum, Clara and Fritz.

❖ ❖ ❖

Mrs. Koch had prepared a lavish holiday meal. Extra tables and chairs were added for the occasion. Ham and platters of sausage, apple stuffing, red cabbage and dumplings, and bowls of creamy potato salad were served to everyone's content. After dinner, the powerful sounds of the trumpet and trombone blended with the more romantic sounds of the flute and French horn, summoning all of the Stahlbaum guests to the grand parlor. This year, Mrs. Stahlbaum included members of the town's Chamber Orchestra for entertainment. The Stahlbaums' piano, which normally sat alone on the balcony, had to share the space this evening.

The orchestra could be heard throughout the Stahlbaums' mansion and down the street, probably to the delight of the Stahlbaums' neighbors. The orchestra continuously played Christmas carols and selections from composers including Bach and Beethoven to Shubert and Mendelssohn.

Dr. Stahlbaum seemed pleased with the Chamber Orchestra. However, they would not be the highlight of the evening. The night was still young and it seemed like magic was in the air. The guests all seemed to feel it, too. At dinner, several guests kept glancing over their shoulders, looking for something that was not there.

The Stahlbaums and their guests were laughing, chatting, singing, and sharing funny stories of events that happened in town earlier in the year. There must have been almost fifty guests, including the children.

Just when the orchestra finished playing a selection, Mrs. Stahlbaum stepped into the center of the room, ushering Clara and a nervous-looking Fritz to the dance floor.

"Everyone, may I have your attention, please," Mrs. Stahlbaum said in a slightly raised voice. Everyone stepped back toward the walls, leaving space in the center of the grand parlor. Mrs. Stahlbaum continued, "This year Clara and Fritz will be leading the waltz."

All of the Stahlbaum guests clapped softly and nodded. The orchestra began playing, and Clara immediately moved to the center of the polished wooden floor.

With everyone watching, Clara stepped out onto the center of the floor with her pink dance slippers. She extended her arms gracefully. She danced, spinning and twirling and gliding across the parlor floor. All the mothers congratulated Mrs. Stahlbaum on how beautifully Clara danced.

The other girls joined Clara and gleefully danced to the precise, staccato sound of the trumpet. All the girls were dressed in colorful party dresses, similar to Clara's. They were all beautiful dancers, almost as good as Clara. They followed behind her, spinning, twirling, and gliding. All the mothers blushed with pride watching their own daughters dance.

After the selection ended, Mrs. Stahlbaum took Fritz by the hand and escorted him to the dance floor. Fritz looked at everyone staring at him.

Stepping toward the center of the parlor floor, Fritz held his free hand to his stomach and looked up at his mother. Mrs. Stahlbaum had a pleasant but determined look on her face. Fritz and Mrs. Stahlbaum were almost at the center of the floor of the grand parlor when the musical selection for the next dance started.

Fritz desperately looked around the room. He looked over at his father. Dr. Stahlbaum was standing near the doorway of the grand parlor next to the great-grandfather clock. Dr. Stahlbaum gave Fritz "the eye." Fritz smiled back at his father and continued to the center of the floor.

Although most of the boys had never taken dance classes, they were taught basic dance steps for social affairs. All the boys followed behind Fritz, shoulders slightly slumped as if they each had hoped Fritz would have found a way to avoid the dance so they wouldn't have to dance either. Only one boy liked to dance, Rupert. He took dance with Miss Patti at the dance academy, along with the girls.

After escorting Fritz to the dance floor, Mrs. Stahlbaum stepped back and joined the other mothers. All the children were now on the dance floor. The girls were lined up on one side with the boys opposite them. Fritz took the hand of Clara's best friend, Marie. He then bowed and off they went, dancing and spinning across the dance floor.

Rupert extended his hand to Clara and bowed. They were next to dance across the floor, joining Fritz and Marie. Each boy and girl followed. Within moments all the children were spinning, twirling, and gliding across the floor. The music changed to a strong rhythmic beat, and the boys danced in a marching style. They seemed to be enjoying the dance as they raised their knees and marched while dancing.

With his eyes on Fritz, Dr. Stahlbaum smiled and whispered to Mrs. Stahlbaum, "Well, I wasn't quite sure you would be able to get him out there."

Mrs. Stahlbaum smiled even though Fritz was doing more marching than dancing.

Dr. Stahlbaum extended his hand to Mrs. Stahlbaum with a bow. They then joined the children on the dance floor in a waltz. The other parents followed. Dr. Stahlbaum's parents were the highlight of the night, so far. All the parents cheered watching Grandma and Grandpa Stahlbaum dance. Everyone was now dancing.

After a short while, Fritz looked around the room at everyone. He then looked at the other boys and they nodded at each other. One by one, the boys slowly eased off the dance floor and slipped into the far corner of the room to play. The boys played and pretended to be soldiers with imaginary bugles and swords.

The girls and all the parents continued dancing to several orchestra selections. As the night passed, the moon glowed even brighter. Everyone seemed to be enjoying the evening–at least for now.

-4-

The Party Continues

Suddenly the music stopped! Clara and the other girls stopped prancing. Fritz and the boys stopped playing. Dr. and Mrs. Stahlbaum and all the other parents stopped dancing. Even Mrs. Koch and Godfrey stopped serving. EVERYTHING STOPPED!

All eyes stared at a black shadow. With his face hidden, a creepy, sinister-looking figure stood motionless at the entrance of the Stahlbaums' grand parlor. The light added to the ominous sight, casting an even larger backdrop on the wall, making it appear to be two figures. The one on the wall was even bigger than the figure in the doorway. With the glowing light of the flickering candles, the shadow on the wall seemed to be moving slowly, slowly, S-L-O-W-L-Y pouncing forward.

"He's here!" recognizing the figure, Dr. Stahlbaum shattered the silence.

One of the ladies shrieked with alarm.

The Stranger was dressed head to toe in black with a swinging black cape draped suspiciously longer than capes were normally worn. His rumpled top hat cast a shadow across his face, distorting it from clear view.

The men looked cautiously at The Stranger, while the women displayed looks of terror. None of the children showed any fear. They looked at The Stranger with wonderment. They didn't even seem put off by the patch that covered The Stranger's left eye. The patch blended seamlessly with The Stranger's attire. It was unclear if the patch was worn because of an eye ailment or as an accouterment to his attire.

Within moments, Dr. Stahlbaum signaled the orchestra to continue playing. Slowly, the musicians began playing while guardedly peeping over the balcony at The Stranger down below. The figure looked even eerier from up above. Although the musicians continued with a selection, caution could be heard through their instruments. "Da da da DAHHHHHHHHH!"

With excited faces, Dr. and Mrs. Stahlbaum rushed across the room to greet The Stranger in black. Their ease seemed to do nothing to make the musicians more comfortable, only more skeptical and uncomfortable. Each seemed to be glad that they were safely positioned on the balcony and not below on the parlor floor.

Then the whispers started. One guest after another began whispering. Their voices were barely audible.

"Who is that stranger? Was he here earlier?"

"I don't remember seeing him at dinner."

"Is that a friend of the Stahlbaums?"

"Hardly. He's probably at the wrong house."

"I do believe I remember seeing him outside earlier when we arrived."

The Stranger stepped out of the doorway and walked across the parlor floor. He met the Stahlbaums in front of the Christmas tree. Although he walked with an air of confidence, he was slightly hunched over.

Extending his hand to The Stranger, Dr. Stahlbaum said gaping, "Dear friend, we have been waiting for your arrival!"

Having moved out of the doorway and away from the wall, The Stranger was no longer casting a shadow. The figure dressed all in black now looked familiar to many of the guests.

The whispers continued, "That looks like—"

"You're right."

"I remember him from last year."

"Oh, yes."

"Yes, the children have been anxious to see you," said Mrs. Stahlbaum to The Stranger.

Clara and Fritz eagerly ran to greet The Stranger. All of their friends followed, eyes gleaming with anticipation.

"Everyone," Dr. Stahlbaum announced, "may I present to you Herr Drosselmeyer!"

The scene in the room changed immediately. The look of dread on the Stahlbaum's guests' faces was now replaced by looks of merriment. The Stahlbaums' guests walked eagerly toward the Christmas tree to greet Herr Drosselmeyer. Laughter again filled the room. The musicians even picked up the beat. They appeared to no longer be spooked by The Stranger.

"Merry Christmas, Uncle Drosselmeyer!" Clara exclaimed.

"Merry Christmas, dear Clara."

"Fritz has been trying to guess all week what you would bring to entertain us this year!"

"You too," Fritz added, as if not wanting to be singled out.

Smiling while bending down to Clara and Fritz with his hands loosely clasped behind his back, Herr Drosselmeyer responded, "And I brought surprises for both of you."

At that moment, Mr. Godfrey directed the house staff to wheel in two enormous boxes. Everyone moved to the side, allowing the boxes to be placed directly in front of the Christmas tree. The boxes, each as tall as Dr. Stahlbaum, were beautifully wrapped in foil paper: one green, and the other wrapped in gold. The opening flaps of the boxes faced the guests and were tied with red velvet ribbon and large bows. The Stahlbaum guests chanted, "Ooh and ahh." Everybody appeared anxious to see what the large boxes contained.

The sound of the orchestra was softer now, as the musicians, once again, were peeping over the balcony, looking down at what was happening in the parlor below.

Fritz screamed, "What's inside, Uncle Drosselmeyer?" He walked around the boxes, examining each. As though the sound would give him a clue, Fritz tapped on each box.

"Fritz!" exclaimed Mrs. Stahlbaum.

"Oh, Mom." Fritz sighed with disappointment as he stepped back from the box. All the children had been listening to every tap with their eyes and mouths wide open, they seemed equally disappointed.

The house staff rested their serving trays and gazed with wonder at the huge gift boxes. Mrs. Koch was the only staff person still working, although she kept a curious eye on the boxes as she picked up half-filled glasses and small dessert plates, some still with slices of fruitcake untouched.

The conductor of the orchestra seized the moment and raised his baton. The orchestra immediately played a dramatic selection, adding to the tension in the parlor. The music was strong and robust, and everyone seemed to be gripping at every sound.

Nobody appeared to notice that Herr Drosselmeyer had moved and was now standing between both boxes, holding the edges of the velvet ribbons that were keeping the boxes closed.

The conductor was now waving his baton madly and the music got louder and *louder*.

Herr Drosselmeyer ceremoniously yanked at the edge of the ribbons untying their bows. Nothing happened. Fritz moved closer. Suddenly the boxes moved.

Fritz jumped back with a shriek. "It moved!"

Everyone was now gawking at the boxes. The flaps on the green box slowly began to open. Everyone jumped back as they watched with their eyes glued to the green box.

Clara gasped. "Something *inside* moved!" Everyone in the parlor stepped back with a yelp, all while keeping their eyes fixed on the green box.

The flaps of the green box continued to open S-L-O-W-L-Y, teasing everyone in the parlor. Nobody moved. The flaps were now half open, hiding what was inside the box.

Then out she stepped: a beautiful doll. The doll looked quite human and was as tall as Clara. Many of the Stahlbaums' guests looked puzzled. The Columbine ballerina doll had an exquisite porcelain face. Only the mechanical eyes that batted stiffly from time to time gave away her secret. She was indeed a doll.

Herr Drosselmeyer reached behind the beautiful Columbine and turned a key. The doll came to life. Everyone in the parlor moved back as the Columbine doll began dancing around the room. She danced to the beat the musicians were playing as if she already knew their selection. But of course, she couldn't, she was just a doll. Even Mrs. Koch put down her serving tray to watch the Columbine ballerina doll.

The Columbine danced brilliantly. All the girls watched in total amazement as the doll swirled and twirled, doing pique turns and pirouettes across the dance floor. Even Fritz and the boys looked charmed by the doll. However, none appeared more enchanted than Clara. Her eyes beamed as she watched the doll's every step. Then all of a sudden, the Columbine doll raised her hands to her lips and blew kisses to everyone. Laughter erupted in the room, and everyone clapped.

"She is amazing!" Clara said.

Clara's best friend Marie acknowledged, "I wish I could dance like that."

"Miss Patti would love to have her in dance class." Clara grinned.

"*Is she really a doll?*" Rupert asked, suspiciously.

All eyes were on the Columbine doll. Nobody seemed to notice that another doll had slowly stepped out of the gold box. The comically dressed Harlequin doll danced over to the Columbine doll.

Everyone laughed at the funny-looking Harlequin. He was very expressive and made faces as he danced. It was obvious that the Harlequin doll was trying to win the affection of the Columbine. However, the Columbine didn't want anything to do with the Harlequin. The show was very entertaining as the dolls danced out their feelings.

The musical selection ended, and at that precise moment, both the Columbine and Harlequin dolls went limp. They stooped over at the waist as if stuck in a bowed position.

"Bravo, Bravo!" said Mrs. Stahlbaum. Everyone joined in, clapping with pleasure.

Looking at Herr Drosselmeyer, Mrs. Stahlbaum said, "This was the best ever. You have really outdone yourself this year."

Dr. Stahlbaum added, "And they look so life-like. How did you—"

Before Dr. Stahlbaum could complete his sentence, Clara interrupted. "Uncle Drosselmeyer, can you make them dance again?"

Fritz broke in and said with disgust, "Can they do anything else?"

"Fritz!" screamed Clara, upset by Fritz's rudeness.

Fritz looked over at Mrs. Stahlbaum. She shot a sharp look in Fritz's direction. Fritz hung his head low and mumbled, "Never mind."

Herr Drosselmeyer responded as he looked at Fritz, "There's more. I have presents for both you and Clara." He then signaled Amalie.

Within moments, Amalie brought two long beautifully-wrapped, normal-sized gift boxes into the parlor. She handed them to Herr Drosselmeyer.

Herr Drosselmeyer bent down to Fritz's height and handed him one of the boxes. "This one is for you, Fritz," Herr Drosselmeyer said. He then handed Clara the other box.

Before Clara could say "thank you," Fritz had torn open the wrapping off his gift and grabbed what was inside. His eyes lit up when he pulled out a shiny, silver sword. Unlike the swords in every toy shop window, this sword was exquisitely detailed and looked real. It appeared heavy because Fritz had to hold it with both hands. The edge, however, was smooth instead of sharp.

Fritz thrust the sword at Rupert's chest and said, "On guard!"

Rupert looked back at Fritz as if glad he didn't have a little brother. The boys quickly wandered back to the far corner of the parlor and pretended to be soldiers.

Hugging her gift box, Clara said, "Thank you, Uncle Drosselmeyer," as if she had won a trophy. The rectangular box was wrapped in red embossed paper and tied with a green satin ribbon. Clara took care untying the ribbon so she could use it for her hair. She then slowly lifted the lid off the box. She first looked confused but then smiled at the gift inside. Her fondness for the gift seemed to grow stronger every second. Her eyes got brighter and her smile wider as she stared inside the box.

Marie asked eagerly, "What is it, Clara? What's in the box?" All of the other girls looked at the box, trying to gain a peek at what was inside.

Everyone watched Clara. Even the musicians were peering over the balcony again, trying to get a look at what was inside Clara's box. The boys even stopped playing and joined everyone around Clara. Mrs. Stahlbaum stood next to Clara and held the box so Clara could remove the gift. Clara looked mesmerized as she pulled the gift out of the box.

Herr Drosselmeyer exclaimed, "It's a Nutcracker Prince doll, Clara!"

The Nutcracker Prince doll was dressed in a red and blue uniform. It had a peculiar face. Not handsome at all, quite the opposite actually. It was so unhandsome it looked endearingly striking. It seemed to captivate everyone, even though it did nothing at all. Even a lever had to be pulled from its backside to crack a nut. Unlike the Columbine and Harlequin dolls that were intricately beautiful and could dance, the Nutcracker Prince doll was stiff, a large wooden toy soldier.

Fritz rushed over. Clara was holding the doll rather tightly and rocking it in her arms. Clara's arm was hiding the doll from Fritz's view. Fritz tugged at Clara's arm. The doll was still hidden from his view, as Clara held the doll tighter. Fritz then grabbed the Nutcracker Prince doll out of Clara's arms.

"Give him back, Fritz!" Clara screamed.

It was too late. Fritz and the other boys were throwing the Nutcracker Prince doll like it was a ball. Fritz looked over at Clara and lowered his eyes. All the boys, except Rupert, were now tossing the Nutcracker doll back and forth. Fritz avoided looking at Mrs. and Dr. Stahlbaum as he ran around the room with the other boys throwing the Nutcracker Prince Doll.

The boys laughed and tossed the Nutcracker Prince doll from boy to boy. Even Dr. Stahlbaum couldn't get the boys to stop. The girls and Clara chased after the boys trying to get the Nutcracker Prince doll back. Clara remembered her birthday party and thought, *here they go again*, as she tried but failed to grab the Nutcracker Prince doll.

The parents chased after their children, trying to stop them from running around the Stahlbaums' parlor like it was a playground. So the parents ran around the parlor, chasing after their children *like it was a playground.*

Mrs. Koch stared scornfully at Mr. Godfrey with a look that said, *"Do something!"* Mr. Godfrey tried to catch the Nutcracker Prince doll and stood holding up his arms and waving them back and forth, like an umpire, in the middle of the parlor, *like it was a playground.*

Mrs. Stahlbaum stared piercingly at Dr. Stahlbaum. Dr. Stahlbaum yelled loudly at Fritz to stop, like a referee, in the middle of the parlor, *like it was a playground.* Dr. Stahlbaum only added to the noise level in the parlor.

Herr Drosselmeyer looked at everyone. His brows were raised as he held up both arms, with his palms raised toward the ceiling.

The conductor and the musicians continued to play their musical selections as they looked down from the balcony at the frenzy below.

Grandma and Grandpa Stahlbaum laughed raucously at the spectacle.

The boys looked to be at the point of endless delirium and continued running, chasing, and tossing the Nutcracker Prince doll. Then it happened.

P-L-O-P!

Although it happened in just seconds, time seemed to stand still. The heads of everyone in the grand parlor followed as the Nutcracker Prince doll fell to the hard wooden floor.

The conductor watched intensely. His body moved lower, in sync with the Nutcracker Prince doll as it fell.

The conductor nearly fell off the balcony when the doll hit the floor. He then quickly composed himself and raised his baton. The orchestra began playing an upbeat selection.

"FRITZ!"

Fritz lowered his head when he heard his father's *I mean business* voice. The other boys quickly walked away, distancing themselves from Fritz.

"I didn't mean to break it, Dad. We were just pla—"

W-H-O-M-P!

That innocent look did not work this time. Fritz got whomped on the butt.

Fritz hung his head and whimpered to a corner of the parlor. The other boys slowly followed after him.

Clara cried as she sat on the floor in the parlor near the Christmas tree. She looked down at her Nutcracker Prince doll as if it were human. Clara's tears fell on the doll's face. She cradled the doll as if trying to relieve its pain. Her Nutcracker Prince doll's jaw was broken.

All the girls surrounded Clara and tried to comfort her.

"I am so sorry, Clara. Let me fix him," Herr Drosselmeyer said sympathetically. He pulled a handkerchief out of his pocket and tied it like a sling around the Nutcracker Prince doll's jaw. "He's going to be just fine now."

Clara smiled as she slowly got up off the floor. She then danced all around the room with her Nutcracker Prince held high in her hands above her head.

For the rest of the night, all the guests danced and laughed. Nobody seemed to notice how late it was until they heard the great-grandfather clock. The musicians then packed their instruments and said their goodbyes. The conductor was the last to leave.

One by one, the Stahlbaum guests each said their goodbyes and headed out into the starry night. As each group left the Stahlbaums' mansion, their shadows seemed to continue to dance in the white snowy landscape under the moonlight.

Dr. Stahlbaum woke up Fritz who had fallen asleep on the floor in a corner of the grand parlor still holding tight to the sword he'd received from Herr Drosselmeyer.

Mrs. Stahlbaum picked up empty glasses and plates alongside Mrs. Koch and Amalie.

Clara sat underneath the tall Christmas tree, wide awake, still gently holding her Nutcracker Prince.

Herr Drosselmeyer was the last of the guests to leave. "Don't worry about me. I'll walk myself out, it looks like your hands are full," he shouted to Dr. Stahlbaum. He walked over to Mrs. Stahlbaum, reached for her hand, and planted a gentle kiss on the back of it.

"You always host the best parties, Katharina."

"Thank you, Herr Drosselmeyer. We all enjoyed your Columbine and Harlequin dolls. And Clara and Fritz always love the gifts you give them. How can a parent compete?" She smiled coyly and gave Herr Drosselmeyer a grand-daughterly kiss on his cheek.

"Okay, I'm off," said Herr Drosselmeyer, as he walked out of the grand parlor.

Mrs. Stahlbaum looked around the parlor. "Where are the Columbine and Harlequin dolls?"

Herr Drosselmeyer didn't answer and continued walking briskly out of the parlor. Mrs. Stahlbaum just shrugged.

"Clara, it's time to go up to bed now," Mrs. Stahlbaum said, as she walked toward the Christmas tree.

"Mother, can I stay up a little bit longer? My Nutcracker Prince feels much better now."

Mrs. Stahlbaum looked down at the Nutcracker Prince doll. Herr Drosselmeyer's handkerchief was gone, and the doll's jaw seemed to be fixed. Mrs. Stahlbaum mumbled, "But how..." She didn't finish her sentence.

Mrs. Stahlbaum continued, "I want you to sleep well tonight, Clara. Tomorrow is Christmas. Leave your Nutcracker Prince doll underneath the Christmas tree."

Clara gently laid her Nutcracker Prince on the toy doll bed she'd gotten as a present from Marie. Clara grabbed her mother's hand and waved good-night to her Nutcracker Prince as she and Mrs. Stahlbaum walked out of the parlor. Over her shoulder, Clara saw that Mrs. Koch was the only person left in the parlor.

Mrs. Koch smiled as she went around the grand parlor blowing out the flames of the oil lamps and candles. She cupped the last candle and was about to blow out the flame.

Suddenly she stopped. With the candlestick shaking in her hand, she extended her arm and jerked the candlestick from side to side, lighting the corners of the room.

The candle's flame cast a shadow across Mrs. Koch's face making it look as though part of her face was no longer there. Her eyes were now wide open and teary. Her eyebrows were in a high arch and her shoulders were raised. Her mouth was open as if she wanted to speak, but nothing came out. Frantically jerking the candlestick, Mrs. Koch looked high and low.

After a few moments, her shoulders relaxed. She stopped jerking the candlestick and turned back toward the door. Her face returned to normal. She then blew out the flame of the last candle. *WHIFF!*

-5-

The Battle

It was midnight and the grand parlor of the Stahlbaums' home was dark, lit only by the moonlight peeping in through the window.

tick-tock...tick-tock...tick-tock...TICK-TOCK...TICK-TICK...TICK-TOCK!

The great-grandfather clock seemed to be pulsating and getting louder with every movement of the swinging pendulum. It seemed to be calling out to someone.

TICK-TOCK...TICK-TOCK...TICK-TOCK!

On top of the great-grandfather clock was a dark shadow, it looked like it had wings. The wings were flapping as the clock called out to someone, but whom?

It started faintly. A screeching-scratching-skittering sound seemed to be coming from behind the walls of the grand parlor. The noise was very distant at first. Then it got louder. *They* were no longer behind the walls. The ticking sound of the great-grandfather clock was no longer the only sound coming from the Stahlbaums' grand parlor.

The screeching-scratching-skittering sound must have scared the moon. As the sounds grew stronger and louder, the glow from the moon seemed to fade. The faint glimmer of moonlight cast a glimpse of moving shadows on the parlor's walls.

As the great-grandfather clock ticked, its last tick marked the midnight hour. Suddenly, the Stahlbaums' Christmas tree seemed to grow taller and taller than its already enormous size. The ceiling in the room appeared to disappear. The festive mood of the parlor earlier in the evening was replaced by an ominous one. The party had definitely ended, and something else was taking over.

A single light was making its way down the Stahlbaums' grand staircase. The light was about four feet above each step, descending at a slow rhythmic pace. Step by step the light descended down the staircase. It then moved across the floor of the foyer. When the light reached the entrance of the parlor, all the screeching-scratching-skittering sounds suddenly stopped. The grand parlor went silent.

Clara entered the parlor. She had awakened after hearing the loud ticking coming from the great-grandfather clock in the parlor. She held her candle's chamber stick holder breast-high so she could see what was making the loud ticking sound. Although she was afraid, she had to check on her Nutcracker Prince. She thought Fritz had probably gone back down to get him.

She did not see Fritz. However, something in the far corner of the room was dark. Her candle was unable to cast light into that corner. The darkness almost looked like a shadow.

Clara's thoughts were interrupted as she glanced over at the tall Christmas tree. It appeared different, much larger. Clara looked down and saw her sweet Nutcracker Prince lying in the little toy bed where she'd left him. She ran to him from across the room, the flame from her candle formed a small tail following behind her.

Clara had the strange sensation that eyes were following her as she ran. She couldn't worry about that, all she thought about was getting to her Nutcracker Prince. She sat at the foot of the toy bed and thought she had never loved anything as much as she loved her Nutcracker Prince. She gently picked him up and rocked him back and forth in her arms. Although his jaw was no longer broken, she rocked him as though he were still injured.

"Sweet Nutcracker Prince, I am going to take care of you," Clara said, talking to the Nutcracker Prince doll. The doll remained stiff. Clara continued, "You won't have to worry about Fritz anymore. I'm going to be sure to keep him away from you."

Clara felt the sensation of eyes staring at her getting even stronger. With the same gentleness that a mother uses to lay down her baby, Clara laid her Nutcracker Prince back in the tiny toy bed. *Fritz must have followed me downstairs*, she thought.

"Fritz," Clara said softly, looking around the room.

Just as Clara turned around, facing the room, the noise stopped. She turned back and looked down at her Nutcracker Prince and then heard it again, a screeching-scratching-skittering sound. She could hear the pit-pattering of claws coming from every corner of the room, except the corner with the dark shadow.

Clara felt trapped, she glanced back at her defenseless Nutcracker Prince and thought she must protect him from what was making those frightful sounds.

Clara stepped to the middle of the room to check for what could be making the sounds. Hearing clawing coming from the tree, she turned back toward her Nutcracker Prince.

"Oh no!" Clara gasped. She saw one of the creatures making the skittering sounds! It was hovering above her defenseless Nutcracker Prince. Clara knew she had to protect her Nutcracker Prince. She gulped.

Clara thought about running upstairs to get her father but knew it would be too late to save her Nutcracker Prince. She would have to be the one to save him. However, she was afraid and wasn't sure she had the courage.

❖ ❖ ❖

Herr Drosselmeyer was hiding in the Stahlbaums' parlor. He sat perched on top of the great-grandfather clock, looking like an old hoot owl flapping his wings. The moon caught a glimpse of Drosselmeyer's pale blue eye, the one not covered by the patch. His eye socket looked completely white as if it didn't hold an eye at all. Like a madman, Drosselmeyer flapped his arms and chanted. He hoped it would work.

❖ ❖ ❖

Clara couldn't believe her eyes. For a moment, she thought this had to be a dream, maybe even a nightmare. However, she could smell the fragrant scent of fresh pine coming from the Christmas tree, letting her know she was not dreaming. This was all real. She closed her eyes, hoping when she opened them, the vision in front of her would be gone.

Clara opened her eyes slowly. The creature had not gone away. She was now face to face with the creature. She couldn't move, she was too afraid to do anything. The creature was bigger than Clara, mud-gray with beady black pebble eyes that stared fiercely into hers, without flinching or blinking. Clara had never been more afraid in all her life.

"This can't be real," Clara shrieked, as she looked into the eyes of the human-sized mouse-looking creature.

Its sharp front teeth protruded beyond its mouth. Standing upright on its hind legs, it didn't seem like a mouse, more like a person. Its belly was large, very large. Clara thought it was probably full of all the people it had eaten.

Her parlor was now full of these mouse creatures. But the one facing her was much bigger than the others. It wore a red cape and jeweled crown. He must be their King, Clara thought.

If he wasn't terrifying enough, his sword sent shivers down Clara's spine. It was shorter than swords

Clara had previously seen, or even Fritz's toy swords, but it was shiny and looked very sharp. The King of the mice gnawed at its front incisors as it stared at Clara.

❖ ❖ ❖

From the top of the great-grandfather clock, Herr Drosselmeyer saw poor Clara and the Mouse King. Clara looked traumatized. Drosselmeyer knew he didn't have much time before the Mouse King would attack Clara.

In one fast move, Drosselmeyer leaped down from the top of the great-grandfather clock. He then rushed over to the Nutcracker Prince doll. The doll was still lying on the toy bed beneath the Christmas tree. Drosselmeyer knew tonight could not be avoided. Not only was Clara's life at stake, but the fate of all the kingdoms deep in the Black Forest. Everything was dependent on what happened next.

❖ ❖ ❖

The mouse creatures surrounded Clara. They all stood upright, gnawing, gnawing, *gnawing* as their black, beady eyes stared at Clara. She looked for an opening between them, but she was completely surrounded. Clara feared she would not be able to escape. And worse, she feared she would not be able to save her Nutcracker Prince.

Then she heard rumbling. It sounded like marching, Clara thought. The mouse creatures must have heard it too because they all looked toward the parlor door. The marching was coming from somewhere upstairs. Clara couldn't be sure, but she thought it was coming out of Fritz's room.

The marching continued, and the sound was now coming down the staircase in the foyer.

❖ ❖ ❖

Herr Drosselmeyer knelt over the toy bed. He draped his cape over the tiny bed, covering it and the Nutcracker Prince doll laying gently on it. Drosselmeyer chanted again. As he chanted, his cape rose. The tiny toy bed grew larger and larger and Drosselmeyer's cape rose higher and higher. The tiny toy bed was now the size of a normal bed. Drosselmeyer bent down over the bed and removed his cape.

Standing next to the bed was a soldier dressed in a red and blue uniform. Clara's Nutcracker Prince doll had come to life.

The Mouse King heard Drosselmeyer's chant and seemed to notice Drosselmeyer for the first time. "I should have destroyed that Nutcracker," sneered the Mouse King. He then dashed toward the Christmas tree, toward the Nutcracker Prince.

❖ ❖ ❖

Clara was relieved to not be eaten alive by the large mouse creature. However, her relief did not last long. Out of the corner of her eye, she saw that the large mouse creature had moved toward the Christmas tree where her Nutcracker Prince lay in his bed. *I will be strong and courageous!* Clara thought to herself, but she was not quite sure what she could do to save her Nutcracker Prince.

The Mouse King looked furious. He charged forward wielding his sword at the Nutcracker Prince.

Clara ran toward the Christmas tree to save her Nutcracker Prince from the king of the mouse creatures. When she got close, she fell back on the parlor sofa at the sight of her Nutcracker Prince, now brought to life. She was astonished. *How can this be?*

"My Nutcracker Prince is a real prince?" Clara thought aloud. She closed her eyes. "This can't be real."

She opened her eyes, expecting to see her Nutcracker Prince back in his tiny toy bed. He was not. The tiny toy bed had disappeared, too. In its place was a bed the same size as her own. The soldier was dressed in the same red and blue soldier uniform her Nutcracker Prince wore. Clara saw he even had a sword at his side, just like her Nutcracker Prince. However, the soldier looked much different. The young soldier was handsome rather than funny-looking like her Nutcracker Prince.

Clara gazed at the soldier quickly. He was almost as tall as her father, with shoulder-length light brown hair that curled slightly at the back of his neck. He had deep blue eyes, the color of sapphire. He was of medium build, not overly muscular. Clara thought he looked to be about the same age as teenage boys from her town, probably not much older than she.

Clara didn't notice that Herr Drosselmeyer was also in the parlor. The marching footsteps continued. Drosselmeyer then swiftly departed, tipping his rumpled hat in the direction of the soldier. Clara still didn't notice him. Nor did she seem to notice when Drosselmeyer left.

Clara looked toward the foyer. The marching was now coming from right outside the parlor door. The Mouse King and his mouse soldiers all stopped. Everyone looked toward the door. *They* were now at the grand parlor and coming in.

"It's a troop of soldiers!" Clara said, surprised. The soldiers were all dressed in the same red and blue uniform as her Nutcracker Prince. Something about them reminded Clara of Fritz's toy soldiers.

The soldiers marched into the room and positioned themselves behind the Nutcracker Prince. He aimed his sword and was ready to do battle against the Mouse King and his mouse soldiers.

The Mouse King's eyes narrowed and his body stiffened when he saw the Nutcracker Prince and soldiers coming toward him. He clenched his teeth and stopped gnawing his incisors. He was breathing so heavily that his chest moved up and down with every breath. He raised his sword and moved threateningly toward the Nutcracker Prince, his troop of mice followed.

The Nutcracker Prince was quick and threw the first strike at the Mouse King, piercing his shoulder with his sword. The Mouse King was knocked off balance, but because of his fur, he was unharmed.

The Nutcracker Prince and the Mouse King fought fiercely. The glint of silver from their swords glimmered as they battled. Clara saw sparks of fire with each strike of the swords. Their swords slashed through the air as they lunged and stabbed.

The Nutcracker Prince's soldiers also had swords. Clara noticed the mouse soldiers did not have swords but were frighteningly nimble. They jumped quickly to avoid being struck by the blades. Instead of swords, the mice used their tails to knock the Nutcracker Prince's soldiers off balance. Having the advantage, the mice would then attack the soldiers.

Clara watched anxiously as the battle between the Nutcracker Prince and the large mouse with the jeweled crown waged on. The soldiers and mice fought hard, but with their sharp swords, the soldiers were winning the battle. The Nutcracker Prince was also winning his fight. Although the Mouse King was fierce, the Nutcracker Prince was focused, with a determined look.

The Mouse King did not relent. The Nutcracker Prince jabbed his sword into the Mouse King. The Mouse King jabbed his sword back at the Nutcracker Prince. They went back and forth until the Nutcracker Prince raised his sword and, in one grand swoop, thrust it into the side of the Mouse King. The Mouse King went down and did not move.

The Nutcracker Prince looked over at Clara. She smiled back at him.

Then it happened. When the Nutcracker Prince was looking over at Clara, the Mouse King used his big tail to knock the Nutcracker Prince off balance. The Nutcracker Prince fell to the floor with a loud thump.

"Aghhh!" Clara screamed.

The Nutcracker Prince's soldiers were also caught off guard, and the mice knocked them down, too. It was swift. In seconds, the soldiers were flat on their backs.

Clara was frantic. When she saw her Nutcracker Prince fall, she jumped off the sofa, no longer paralyzed by fear. She was determined to save her Nutcracker Prince. She tried to move past the mouse soldiers, but they kept her from getting close to the Nutcracker Prince and the Mouse King.

Clara jumped on the bed and tried to jump over the mice. The mice laughed hysterically at her. With Clara on it, the mice slid the bed back and forth all across the polished floor of the parlor. Clara held tight to the bed post to avoid falling off. Tears welled up in her eyes.

The Mouse King snorted and laughed as he watched Clara being tossed around the room in the bed. After a short while, he grunted. The mice stopped. He then knelt down above the Nutcracker Prince and raised his sword.

"No!" Clara screamed as she looked around desperately for a weapon. Clara sighed in despair, the only thing she had were her slippers. Clara took off one of her slippers and threw it at the Mouse King. Watching Clara, the Mouse King laughed loudly and pretended to be hurt by the slipper.

Suddenly, the Mouse King fell to his knees. He held the blade that had gone through his chest. Clara had distracted him long enough for the Nutcracker Prince to raise his sword and thrust it into the heart of the Mouse King.

With that fatal strike, the battle was over.

Standing erect on their hind legs, the mice ran around in circles waving wildly. With their tails dragging between their legs, they finally picked up their dead king and carried him out of the parlor.

The soldiers rejoiced.

Clara couldn't believe everything that had just happened. She went over to the parlor door after all the mice departed. They were gone. The mice vanished! There was no trace of the Mouse King or his troop of mouse soldiers. GONE!

Clara turned back around. All the soldiers dressed in red and blue uniforms had now disappeared, too! DISAPPEARED!

In his beaten-up red and blue uniform, the Nutcracker Prince stood in the center of the parlor and smiled at Clara.

"Clara, it's me."

Like a big brother, the Nutcracker Prince took Clara by the hand and walked her over to the large picture window behind the tall Christmas tree. "I have something for you, Clara."

The Nutcracker Prince pulled a crystal necklace from underneath his uniform and put it around Clara's neck. "This crystal will keep you warm deep in the Black Forest. Egon will be coming after us. We must go now!"

Clara looked around the grand parlor. She wondered if she would ever see her home again. She then turned back around and looked out of the large picture window. SNOW.

"The stars glimmered like lightning bugs in the night sky."

ACT 2

-6-

Snow

Clara's eyes were closed and her heart was pounding. The last thing she saw was the pure white snow on the ground below when the Nutcracker Prince opened her parlor room window. *Is this really my Nutcracker Prince? Did he really come to life?* Clara wondered.

Surely they should have hit the ground below by now, Clara thought, waiting to hit the cold dampness of the snow. However, it didn't appear they were falling at all.

It felt as though they were almost flying. Not actually flying like the white-tailed eagles she saw when they visited her Uncle Drosselmeyer. No, she and her Nutcracker Prince were not flying like eagles. But they weren't falling either. Clara kept anticipating the coldness of the snow and had little hope that the small crystal necklace would keep her warm. However, she was warm.

"Clara, you can open your eyes." The Nutcracker Prince chuckled as he looked at Clara with her eyes closed tight, as if the tighter she clenched her eyes the more she was protected from what she could not see. Clara slowly opened her eyes, not knowing what to expect.

"Let me formally introduce myself. I am Prince Dustin Egbert Conrad von Konig of Konfetenburg. Most everyone calls me Prince Dustin."

Clara looked all around, they were definitely flying or something, she figured. Not feeling at all comfortable yet compelled by impulses beyond her control, Clara stared at the snow far below as she responded, "Hi, uh. I'm uhm..."

"I know your name is Clara," Prince Dustin acknowledged as he smiled at her.

She muttered softly, "Clara." Still gazing down at the snow below, she added trembling, "Yes, Clara, that's my name."

Prince Dustin laughed. "We're not going to fall. You don't have to be afraid."

Clara didn't respond. She just looked at Prince Dustin with a cautious side-glance and continued to grip his hand tightly.

Clara thought back to the events of the evening starting with her brother Fritz being in her bedroom. She remembered stepping into one of her dance slippers and feeling something furry inside her shoe. It had felt like a cotton ball, she remembered. When she bent down to remove it, Fritz's pet mouse stared back at her with its protruding black beady eyes and some crumbled gingerbread on its pointed snout. When she screamed, the mouse jumped out of her slipper and ran down the hallway.

Clara knew that of all of her fears, she feared mice the most. The small little creatures could lurk anywhere, out of sight. She shuddered when she thought about their long scaly tails.

Clara recalled everything else that had happened that evening. Fritz and his little mouse seemed so long ago. His little mouse didn't seem so scary at all to Clara now. She wondered how she was ever afraid of such a small little creature, especially now that she knew there were much bigger creatures, bigger mice. She thought about *those* mouse creatures. *Are they following us?* Clara wondered.

"My kingdom is deep in the Black Forest. The people who live in the Black Forest refer to it as the Land of Sweets," Prince Dustin said matter-of-factly.

Clara inquired, "Why do they call it the Land of Sweets?"

"Because our rivers are made of chocolate, and gumdrops hang from the trees," Prince Dustin said.

Clara smiled after she caught on that Prince Dustin was just joking.

Prince Dustin explained, in a more serious tone, "We have the best bakers of all the kingdoms in the Black Forest. They bake the best gingerbread, with sweet white creamy icing, and plum cake sprinkled with cinnamon and sugar. They bake all kinds of bread and drop them off every morning at everyone's door."

He continued, "Because everyone started calling our kingdom the 'Land of Sweets,' the bakers started making candy, too. Candy canes, sugarplums, chocolate bonbons, and even gumdrops."

Prince Dustin managed to allay Clara's fears somewhat by telling her about his kingdom, however, she squeezed his hand a little tighter after looking down at the forest below. Prince Dustin must have sensed Clara was frightened. He gave her a reassuring squeeze back.

Clara wondered what time it was. The stars glimmered like lightning bugs in the night sky. The trees on the ground below were dense and were flocked by snow. The mountains seemed close although they were far away. Clara and Prince Dustin were traveling in the blue-black abyss of the night sky above the Black Forest.

"We won't be able to fly the entire way," Prince Dustin commented. "My kingdom is deep in the Black Forest. We will have to journey down the river, and then we will rest at Queen Nordika's Ice Palace until I regain my full strength. We have to travel with haste because the Mouse King's brother, Egon, will not be far behind."

"Is he able to fly, too?" Clara asked.

"No. But the mice people are very swift, which is why we will have to move quickly once we land. Had you not distracted the Mouse King with your slipper, I wouldn't have had the strength to continue fighting.

We might not be so lucky next time. The Mouse King's brother will be coming with a vengeance. The news may not have made it back to Egon yet, but it will soon," Prince Dustin lamented.

"What about your parents?" Clara asked, wondering why Prince Dustin hadn't mentioned them.

"My father was, or is, King Marc Friedrich Graf von Konig and my mother is Queen Arabelle," Prince Dustin started. "They left to explore faraway lands and never returned. It's assumed they were killed by one of the creatures that live deep in the Black Forest. I'm not sure, though. There are places even deeper in the Black Forest than my kingdom. The Black Forest has places that are very dangerous."

Clara shuddered at the thought and didn't want to know anything more. Her experiences with the Black Forest, thus far, were scary enough.

Clara changed subjects. "Do you have any brothers or sisters?"

"I was an only child until my parents adopted a little girl. My sister is two years younger than me. She was one of the few survivors when her kingdom fell under attack by the Kingdom of the Mice. The people of her kingdom were very peaceful and had not experienced war for many centuries, so they were not prepared for the attack," Prince Dustin replied.

He went on to explain how his father, King Marc, had traveled to the Kingdom of Fliegen to provide assistance. However, when King Marc and his soldiers arrived, it was already too late. The kingdom was up in flames by a surprise attack. Most of the people had fled or perished. They were about to return to Konfetenburg when his father, King Marc, heard a baby's cry from underneath a brush. Under the brush they found a baby girl bundled up in a small bassinet.

"When my father returned, my mother immediately brought the baby girl into our castle and she became a member of our family," Prince Dustin added. "My sister was named Princess Leyna. However, everyone calls her Sugar Plum or Princess Sugar Plum."

"I like her name, Princess Sugar Plum," Clara exclaimed.

Clara glanced at the forest below and thought how beautiful the Black Forest was with its seemingly endless trees. It was lush even in winter. The tall green pine trees were so dense that, from above, nothing on the ground could be seen through the trees, making the forest below a canopy of blackness.

Prince Dustin said, "I have flown to this area many times with Princess Sugar Plum."

Clara nodded.

"We had heard rumors that my father and mother might have traveled along the river, so we searched this location for clues. However, we were never able to find any traces of them."

Clara closed her eyes again when she felt they were descending. It was a gradual descent, not a quick free-fall from the sky, however, she was still afraid. She kept her eyes tightly shut and then thought about how it seemed to have been a while since they had jumped from her parlor window. She reasoned that if they were going to fall, they would have done so by now, so she decided to peek as they descended. Clara slowly opened her eyes and squeezed Prince Dustin's hand tightly.

My Nutcracker Prince is a real prince, Clara acknowledged with a smile. She looked at Prince Dustin from the corner of her eyes. She had too many questions. Somehow, she couldn't open her mouth to ask even one. She just kept looking at the trees. The sharp needles of the evergreens were getting closer and closer as they descended.

Looking down at the snow flocked evergreens, Clara noticed she was still wearing her pajamas with her ruffled pantaloons. The gown was made of soft cotton. The balloon sleeves had red ribbons that tied into bows right below her elbow. The bow on her right sleeve had become untied. She looked farther down and noticed she was wearing only one slipper. She was glad she had put her slippers on in her bedroom when she heard the loud ticking coming from the parlor. But now she panicked. *How am I going to walk in the snow with only one slipper?* she worried.

Clara glanced over at Prince Dustin to tell him about the dilemma. However, before she could open her lips, she saw her other slipper in Prince Dustin's pocket. She figured he must have grabbed it after she threw it at the Mouse King. With her free hand, she pulled the crystal necklace from underneath her gown. It *did* keep her warm. She wasn't cold at all.

"The Black Forest is very different from my hometown," Clara said to Prince Dustin as she slipped the crystal necklace back underneath her gown.

"Only the lands that are *deep in the Black Forest*," responded Prince Dustin. "Although we only traveled for a short period, we were actually traveling at a very fast pace." He added, "When you fly, it is so smooth that it doesn't feel like you are moving at all. An hour has not yet passed since midnight."

Talking about the time made Clara think back to earlier in the evening when she was at home. She remembered the party and dancing with her friends. She thought about her Uncle Drosselmeyer and the beautiful dancing Columbine doll and funny Harlequin. She thought about her Grandmamma and Grandpapa. Even for their age, they were splendid dancers.

Clara thought about her mother and father. Her father always checked on her and tucked her in after she went to bed. He had already tucked her in for the night, so he might not know she was no longer in her bed. She wondered what her mother would do when she found out Clara had not slept in her bed all night.

And poor Fritz. Clara sighed. Every Christmas morning, before running downstairs to open presents, Fritz would come to her room, jump on her bed, and wake her up. *He probably would feel bad that he put his little pet mouse in my slipper*, Clara thought sadly.

They were at the tops of the evergreen trees now. Clara wondered how they would get through the trees. She couldn't see anything but sharp pine needles sticking out of the snow-covered branches. Clara looked at the needles. She closed her eyes and squeezed Prince Dustin's hand even tighter. With her free hand, Clara crossed her fingers.

Prince Dustin turned slightly left to a small opening in the trees. "Clara, you can open your eyes. You should be able to see the river now. It's over to the right. We're going just beyond the river's bend."

Clara, still thinking about the sharp evergreen needles, opened her eyes slightly and peeked. Yes, they had been sailing through the skies and were about to land. She saw a magnificent river ahead, the light from the moon that made it through the trees cast a soft glow against the river's water and flickered shades of indigo, purple, and gold. With the soft wind, the river surfed the wave.

The snow covered the ground all around and lit up the area. Beyond the river's bend, Clara could see a clearing, a path. They were moving in that direction. They landed at a rock near the river's edge right at the beginning of the path. Clara wondered what animal or creature made the path in the snow. Prince Dustin looked at her and lifted her just before they landed. He set her down on top of a large rock. Clara was glad her bare foot had not stepped on the cold snow. If it was cold, she wasn't sure because she still felt warm, a comfortable warm. Prince Dustin pulled her slipper out of his pocket and gently placed it on her foot.

Prince Dustin looked into Clara's big brown eyes and proclaimed, "We are now *deep in the Black Forest*."

-7-

Journey down the River – Part One

"Deep in the Black Forest?" Clara whispered, trying not to be heard by any nearby creatures.

Prince Dustin replied, "Yes, Clara. Life deep in the Black Forest is much different than your hometown."

"Like the mouse creatures?" Clara grimaced, remembering the human-sized mice that attacked her in her parlor. "Different for sure."

"The inhabitants here live very long lives and have had little or no interaction with anything outside the Black Forest. To us, our lives are normal," Prince Dustin responded calmly. "Things here can seem scary, I suppose. My parents have traveled outside the Black Forest, and when I was younger, they told me no place can surpass the beauty of the Black Forest. Our trees are much bigger and greener, even in winter." Prince Dustin pointed with pride to the enormous pine and spruce conifer trees that lined the river's bank.

"The forest is so heavily populated with trees that even in the daytime, very little light can penetrate through the foliage," Prince Dustin said. "It's always serenely dark and majestic in the Black Forest. The only areas that get light are near the rivers or in areas where the trees have been cleared."

Clara nodded as she looked around. "We always get our Christmas trees from the Black Forest. My mother says that at Christmas time 'the whole house should smell like evergreen,' so she has Mr. Baumgartner find us the biggest tree every year." Clara took a whiff of air. "It smells like this in our house every Christmas!"

Clara and Prince Dustin were surrounded by huge trees. The trees were much larger than any trees Clara had ever seen. She knew they had to be much deeper in the forest than she had ever gone. Possibly to the place the cottage people spoke about. A place nobody was ever known to have visited, or at least never came back to talk about. Clara thought anxiously, the place of the legends.

The trunks of some of the trees were as much as ten feet wide. Clara knew that even if she could extend her arms out twice, she still could not touch the entire base of some of the trees. She didn't want to think about the creatures that could be lurking behind those trees. She would never see them until it was too late, she thought.

Clara wished she were back in her cozy bed. She remembered her mother taking her to her bedroom. She had quickly put on her gown and pantaloons and wanted to go to sleep fast so she could wake up to see her Nutcracker Prince. Her father came in a few moments later and tucked her in bed and then lit the logs in her fireplace. She remembered him saying, "Sweet dreams, dear Clara. Tomorrow is Christmas day."

Clara glanced at Prince Dustin. His confident look made her feel a little better. She was with the Nutcracker Prince. Earlier that night, he did slay the–Mouse King, Clara reasoned. Clara remembered that Prince Dustin had called the mouse creature with the robe and crown, the Mouse King. She certainly hoped none of the Mouse King's soldiers were hiding behind the trees.

The tops of the trees were so high in the sky that Clara thought even if it was daytime and the sun was shining, she would still not be able to see the tops of the trees from down where they were. She thought back to when she and Prince Dustin were sailing across the sky, when she peeked out, the tops of the trees seemed to almost be able to touch the stars in the sky.

Clara remembered seeing a tree that tall: the tree in her grand parlor after the Christmas party when she went back down after hearing the ticking sound. She remembered thinking how she could no longer see the ceiling. The Christmas tree had grown and was much taller. It continued beyond what she was able to see. Clara shook her head. *That couldn't have been possible.*

Prince Dustin said, "This is the River Stromabwarts. We consider all things to be living, of life, so everything in the Black Forest has a name."

Clara nodded.

"We will take that path," Prince Dustin added in a serious tone as he pointed to the path along the river. "We must hurry to get there!"

"I'm right beside you," Clara said, jumping up off the rock. She sensed fear in Prince Dustin's voice for the first time. *Why are we in a hurry?* she thought. She started to ask but then decided she really didn't want to know the answer. Not at that moment, anyway. She just wanted to quickly get to *there*, wherever there was.

The path was barely wide enough for them to walk side by side, touching shoulders. In some spots, they had to walk single file. Prince Dustin made sure to walk behind Clara when the path narrowed. Clara was glad she had both of her dance slippers and was not walking with one bare foot. Even though the crystal kept her warm, it would not have provided her any protection from the ground.

As they walked down the river's path, Clara kept both eyes wide open. All around her she heard noises from behind the trees. Some noises she recognized but many she did not. She recognized the sound of hoot owls, which seemed to be everywhere on the tree limbs above them. At first, she looked up at every hoot, but after they had been walking for a while, the hoots became part of the ever-present background noise, and she no longer heard them.

Noise was coming from the river, too. There were definitely fish or something swimming around in the water. Every once in a while she heard the sound of a large splash. Whatever was in the river, *it* seemed to be going in the same direction they were going. *Is it following us?* Clara wondered.

After they had been walking for a while, Prince Dustin said, "We're going just ahead. Many years ago, some of the trees were chopped down leaving the stumps."

Clara nodded.

When they reached the clearing, Prince Dustin asked Clara if she was tired. She shook her head no. She thought how she was too afraid to think about being tired. However, now that it was mentioned, all of a sudden, she felt tired.

"Maybe we can take a short break anyway because we still have a long way to go," Prince Dustin said.

Clara noticed the worried look on Prince Dustin's face. "Thank you for saving me from that mouse creature," Clara said with sincerity.

"*You* saved us, Clara! By distracting the Mouse King, I was able to catch him off guard."

Clara half-smiled, she didn't feel like she had done much of anything at all.

"I have not regained my full strength since being returned to a prince by the great wizard Drosselmeyer."

Surprised by this statement, Clara responded, "Drosselmeyer? *My* Uncle Drosselmeyer?"

"Yes," Prince Dustin replied.

"My Uncle Drosselmeyer is a wizard?"

Prince Dustin seemed surprised, "You didn't know?"

Clara shook her head.

Prince Dustin told her how he was turned into the toy Nutcracker Prince doll by Drosselmeyer to protect him from the Mouse King. The Mouse King was planning to attack Prince Dustin's kingdom. One of Prince Dustin's lieutenants had intercepted a message alerting them of the attack. He and his sister, Princess Sugar Plum, decided their army should strike the Mouse King first before the mice made it to his kingdom in the Land of Konfetenburg. Princess Sugar Plum was to remain at their castle while he and their army went off to battle the Mouse King and his troops.

"Princess Sugar Plum is from the Land of the Fliegen," Prince Dustin interjected, somewhat off topic. He then gave Clara a quick glance. "Do you understand, Clara?"

Clara just nodded.

"My parents have been gone for a few years now. My sister, Princess Sugar Plum, and I are the reigning monarchs until my fifteenth birthday. By decree, on my fifteenth birthday, I become King of Konfetenburg," Prince Dustin elaborated.

Clara responded, "Is that why the Mouse King attacked you?"

"Yes," Prince Dustin said. "The Mouse King wanted to slay me before I reached my fifteenth birthday. By my death, there would be no king or queen. Eventually, my kingdom would no longer exist."

"What about Princess Sugar Plum?" Clara asked.

"Sugar Plum, by decree, is not able to hold the title of Queen since she was adopted. She can only be a princess. If she has children, they can hold the title of Prince or Princess, not King or Queen either. Only a person with a direct bloodline can be crowned king or queen of Konfetenburg. Eventually, my kingdom would dissolve or be taken over without a ruling king or queen."

"My father, King Marc, protected many of the other kingdoms in the Black Forest from attacks by the Mouse King. On my fifteenth birthday, when I become king, it will become my duty to protect the other kingdoms," Prince Dustin said proudly. "That is why the Mouse King wanted me dead. He knew I would soon be a threat to him and his kingdom."

Clara nodded and then asked with a raised voice, "And why were you turned into a Nutcracker Prince doll?"

"When we were on our way to attack the Mouse King, Drosselmeyer went to Konfetenburg to warn us that the Mouse King had changed his plans. The Mouse King now planned to raid the Land of Sweets a day earlier than we expected," explained Prince Dustin.

"Princess Sugar Plum informed Drosselmeyer that I had already left for battle and there would be nobody to lead the charge against a surprise attack at Konfetenburg."

"To avoid an ambush in Konfetenburg, Drosselmeyer leaked a message to the Mouse King that I was no longer there."

"Drosselmeyer then came to our campsite and warned us that the Mouse King and his full army were now on their way to attack me and my soldiers in the forest. Drosselmeyer told me how he was able to avert an attack at my castle but wouldn't be able to stop an attack in the forest."

"We had not planned for a full out war against the Mouse King. My soldiers were divided. Some were still at the castle. With a divided army, I would have been unable to defend against an attack from the Mouse King's full army."

"To avoid the battle, I sent my troops back to the castle and Drosselmeyer turned me into the Nutcracker Prince doll." Prince Dustin elaborated.

Clara sighed. "The Black Forest is very different from my hometown."

"I was to remain a doll until my fifteenth birthday. At fifteen, I would be King and also have control of all the armies of the nearby kingdoms. The Mouse King would be helpless against a united assault."

"Drosselmeyer spoke of a girl in the town outside the Black Forest who loved dolls and always handled the toys he gave her with great care. He thought the Mouse King would not venture out of the Black Forest to look for me. He decided to give you the Nutcracker Prince doll. He thought I would be safe from the Mouse King until I turned fifteen," Prince Dustin added.

"But the Mouse King must have found out?" Clara questioned.

"Yes, that is why he was in your parlor," Prince Dustin said. "He planned to destroy the Nutcracker Prince doll before my fifteenth birthday so that Drosselmeyer could not turn me back into a prince, and I would never become King." Prince Dustin added solemnly.

Prince Dustin continued, "Egon is his brother. He is even more evil than the Mouse King. He will be coming after us for revenge. You are not safe as long as Egon is alive."

Clara shuddered.

SPLISH-SPLASH

Clara heard a loud splash coming from the river. She had heard the splashing before. Whatever was swimming down the river was definitely following them because *it* should have been farther down the river by now since they had stopped to rest. Clara thought Prince Dustin must have heard it too because he looked at the river suspiciously.

SPLISH-SPLASH

SPLISH-SPLASH SPLISH-SPLASH!

It found them.

Prince Dustin jumped up quickly and shouted, "We have to leave *now!*"

-8-

Journey down the River – Part Two

The sounds from the forest were now very loud. The animals of the night had awakened.

It was pitch black as Clara and Prince Dustin continued down the path. Clara looked into the darkness of the pine trees and was glad they were walking alongside the river's bank.

She peered into the wall of evergreen trees, but everything was dark. Without any reflection of light, even the snow looked black deep in the Black Forest.

The forest was dark but not silent. Sounds were coming from beyond the blackness of the trees. Clara heard animals that she couldn't see, they climbed up the trees as she and Prince Dustin approached.

Creatures were prowling, waiting to pounce, Clara imagined. She didn't know if she should be more afraid of the river, with the loud splashing sounds from time to time, or the forest. She figured that with the moonlight on the river, she could at least see anything that came after them.

Clara was too afraid to say anything to Prince Dustin. She wanted to ask him about all the noises but didn't want to attract the attention of any animals or creatures. The noises that had seemed to fade into the background were very loud now. They were no longer background noise. The animals seemed to want their presence to be known.

Clara heard a cry. She remembered hearing that sound before when she visited her Uncle Drosselmeyer. It sounded like a baby. The cry was coming from several directions. Clara knew which animal made that sound and hoped not to cross paths with it tonight.

Although Clara had a lot more questions she wanted to ask Prince Dustin, she remained silent. The only sound they made was the squishing sound of their shoes each time they took a step in the snow. Even so, Clara was walking lightly, she didn't want the animals *or creatures* to hear even that.

SPLISH-SPLASH SPLISH-SPLASH!

It was still following them, Clara bemoaned.

"Up ahead, there should be a small boat," Prince Dustin stated. "I left it there when I was searching for my parents. Sugar Plum and I had sought counsel with the Snow Queen, I mean, Queen Nordika. She directed us to lands far beyond the river. She said if they were still alive, they had most likely been abducted."

"So your parents *may* still be alive?" Clara asked.

Prince Dustin lowered his head. "It is not likely. However, there's still hope. Queen Nordika—"

"The Snow Queen? You mentioned that name before," Clara interjected.

"Yes. Everyone calls Queen Nordika the Snow Queen. She lives in the Ice Palace." Prince Dustin continued, "She has scouts that stay well-informed of everything that happens in the Black Forest. However, there are some areas that go even *deeper* in the Black Forest. Even Queen Nordika is not aware of what happens in those territories. Those territories are quite wicked. We hope my parents didn't journey to those places."

Clara asked, "Is that where the Mouse King lives, I mean, lived? His brother, Egon. I mean where Egon lives?"

Prince Dustin responded solemnly, "No, Clara. There are creatures much more dangerous than the Mouse King and even Egon."

Clara gasped, "I hope we don't run across any of them."

"The boat should be underneath that fallen tree, right next to the river," Prince Dustin said as he pointed ahead. He tugged at the helm of the small boat and pulled it from underneath the tree. Tall grass, now wheat-brown and dead, had grown around it. After a few more tugs, it was free of the tree. Clara looked at the boat and thought it was quite small. She then thought about the creature making the *SPLISH-SPLASH* sounds in the river and thought that if the creature attacked them, the boat was so small it would capsize.

Prince Dustin pulled the boat onto the edge of the river and signaled for Clara to join him. Although Clara was reluctant to get inside the small boat for fear of the creature *SPLISH-SPLASHING* in the river, she trusted Prince Dustin. She also didn't want to continue walking down the path and be confronted by the creatures making the loud noises behind the trees. She had to face her fears. Actually, she knew they had no other choice.

Clara hopped into the small boat. It had two benches. Prince Dustin directed her to the front bench. Clara sat on it facing backward so that she could easily speak with Prince Dustin while traveling down the river.

Prince Dustin launched the boat into the river. The boat jerked from side to side. *SWOOSH! SWOOSH!* Prince Dustin jumped in as Clara held tight to the sides of the rowboat. Anchors aweigh and off they went, down the murky River Stromabwarts.

After a while, Clara felt more comfortable in the boat, the river was so still that had Prince Dustin not been rowing, the boat would not have moved at all. Whatever *it* was that had been making the *SPLISH-SPLASH* sounds in the river had either stopped following them or was no longer close. They hadn't heard the splashing sounds since they got into the boat, Clara thought with relief.

Facing Prince Dustin, Clara couldn't see what was ahead of them unless she turned around. She noticed Prince Dustin looked relaxed now. His shoulders were not fully erect as they had been earlier, and his expression was not so intense. He was actually smiling as he rowed the boat, Clara noticed.

"You must have a lot of questions, Clara."

Clara smiled. "Not really." Actually, she did have a lot of questions. She just didn't want Prince Dustin to know how scared she really was, by asking all her questions. She wanted him to think she was comfortable and not afraid. "I do have one question."

"Ask away."

"Were we really flying? I remember you taking my hand and jumping out of the window in my parlor. People don't actually fly, not in my hometown, anyway."

Prince Dustin chuckled. "Yes, we were flying."

"But how—"

Prince Dustin interrupted, "Remember I told you that Princess Sugar Plum was from the Land of Fliegen?"

Clara twisted her lip, not quite knowing what that had to do with anything.

"Well, the people of Fliegen are all Tree Fairies."

Clara hesitated. "Tree Fairies?"

"Yes, Tree Fairies. Tree Fairies fly."

Even more confused, Clara said slowly, "But you're not a Tree Fairy. *Are you?*"

Prince Dustin stopped rowing the boat to explain. "No, I am not. In the Land of the Tree Fairies, there is a

Great Tree. The tree can give a person the power to fly. A Tree Fairy has to ask the tree to give a person the power and tell the tree why the person should have this power."

"If the Great Tree agrees, the person will have the power to fly. After our parents had been gone for a while, Sugar Plum took me to the Great Tree and told the tree that my parents had adopted her after her village had been attacked by the Mouse King. She also told the tree that my parents, her adopted parents, had disappeared. She explained to the Great Tree that she wanted me to have the power to fly so I could search for our parents in areas I wouldn't be able to reach on foot."

"Were you able to fly then?" Clara asked.

"Yes, the Great Tree granted me the power to fly."

Clara was quiet while she thought about all Prince Dustin had shared. After pondering her thoughts, she said, still not fully understanding, "Hmmm, but I was flying, too."

Prince Dustin picked up the oars and started rowing as he laughed. "*You* were not actually flying, Clara."

"Huh?"

"My energy force was keeping you up in the sky with me. I didn't have to hold your hand, my energy would have kept you up within a certain distance."

"But you held my hand, so you held me up?"

"Uh, well—I knew you were afraid. I held your hand so you wouldn't think you were going to fall," Prince Dustin said.

"I wasn't afraid." Clara and Prince Dustin both laughed at Clara's comment. "Well, maybe a little," Clara chuckled.

Clara smiled and looked at the river behind Prince Dustin. Although the moon lit the water close around them, the river behind them was jet black. The river far behind them blended in with the forest. The farther Clara looked back, the more everything just looked like a continuous black canvas. She turned around so she was able to see in front of her, in the direction they were going. It was pitch black, too. *There* was probably still far away, Clara thought.

"Can we fly to where we're going?" she asked.

"Since I am not a Tree Fairy, flying makes me very weak. I only fly if I need to get somewhere fast. Or if I need to go somewhere I cannot travel to easily on foot or by animal. I also have not fully gained my strength back from being turned back into a Prince. My strength will have to build back up before I am able to fly again."

"Aghhh," Clara exclaimed.

SPLISH-SPLASH   SPLISH-SPLASH-SPLASH   SPLISH-SPLASH SPLISH-SPLASH!

Clara heard *It* again. *It* was still following them. She looked frantically behind the boat for *It*. Prince Dustin rowed faster. She wanted to ask Prince Dustin if he had heard *It*, but she didn't want to know his answer. She wanted to believe that maybe *It* was just a tree limb or something that had fallen into the river.

They both remained quiet as Prince Dustin rowed the boat down the river. Clara gripped the sides of the boat tightly as she looked up at the stars. Whatever *It* was, she didn't want to see it.

The sounds coming from the forest seemed louder now. Clara heard every hoot, cry, and howl. She wondered how long it would take for them to get *there* but was too afraid to ask for fear of her voice being heard by any nearby creatures. They continued down the river.

They traveled farther and farther down the river, and Clara had not heard any splashing sounds for a while. She tried to convince herself that it must have been a tree limb she heard earlier. She was feeling somewhat at ease again, or at least not as afraid as she was when she heard the splashing sound.

At one stretch of the river, it narrowed. The hoots, cries, and howls had again blended into the background. The stars from the sky shone down on the tops of the nearby pine trees that flanked the river. Clara was able to see the snow flocking the evergreen trees. She then pulled the crystal necklace from underneath her gown and wondered how the crystal was able to keep her warm. She then tucked it back.

"Are we almost *there*?" Clara asked.

"We don't have *too* much farther to go."

Clara thought about how Prince Dustin emphasized *too*. She figured they probably had much farther to go than Prince Dustin wanted to say.

Clara thought about the horrible mouse creatures that attacked her in her parlor. She thought about their king and how Prince Dustin slew him with his sword. Prince Dustin had his sword at his side in a leather sheath. Clara noticed he had not taken it off even inside the boat.

Looking at Prince Dustin, Clara asked, "And what did you say is the name of the Mouse King's brother? Uh—"

"Egon."

"Yes, Egon. Do you think he will find us?" Clara asked.

Prince Dustin immediately stopped rowing and looked directly at Clara. His eyes narrowed and his face became distorted. "Clara, I don't want to frighten you, but Egon will not stop until he finds us. He will not sleep, he will not eat, and yes, he will find us."

Clara's face dropped.

Prince Dustin grabbed the oars and continued rowing. Clara noticed that Prince Dustin was rowing much faster and he seemed to be focused on the river ahead. With every pull of the oars, he was getting them closer.

Clara thought about Prince Dustin's comments that Egon would find them. She was worried about Prince Dustin, her Nutcracker Prince. Prince Dustin must have felt her staring and anxiously glanced directly at her. She felt his eyes. She continued to look up at the night sky, she didn't want Prince Dustin to see the fear in her eyes.

The river widened as they journeyed downstream. Except for the stars and the moon, everything was pitch black: the sky above, the water below, and the forest beyond. Then—

WHOMPPPPPPPPPP!

Something slammed into the bottom of their boat, almost toppling it over. *It* had caught up to them!

-9-

River Encounter with *It*

"Hold on, Clara!"

"What was that? Was *It* Egon?"

"It might strike again. Crouch down in the bottom of the boat and hold on!"

"I can't see anything in the river!" Clara screamed. "Is *It* coming back?"

"I don't know! Just hold on tight, Clara!"

Clara's heart was pounding in her chest as she firmly gripped the sides of the rowboat. She looked frantically back and forth for *It*. Nothing. The murky water hid the creature that had been following them since they reached the river.

Prince Dustin unsheathed his sword and half stood. His eyes keenly looked for any movement in the water.

Prince Dustin pointed his sword up and forward. Clara looked up at Prince Dustin in his red and blue uniform. He no longer looked like her Nutcracker Prince. He reminded her of pictures she had seen in books of soldiers about to go to battle. His long, sharp silver sword glimmered in the moon's light. She hoped that whatever it was that had attacked them was scared away by Prince Dustin.

The water was quiet again. Clara could hear the hoots, cries, and howls coming from the forest. The noises from the animals in the forest never actually stopped. Clara just stopped focusing on *those* sounds. Still crouched at the bottom of the rowboat, she looked over the boat's side into the forest. Somewhere out there was Egon. Clara trembled as she thought back to the Mouse King and how he'd looked at her, gnawing his razor-sharp teeth. Clara hoped Prince Dustin was wrong. She hoped Egon would not find them.

Except for the hooting owls, all was quiet. The crying and howling had stopped. Whatever was making those sounds either went farther into the forest or was quietly watching them. Prince Dustin stayed ready for a while, holding his sword high. After what seemed like a long time, he finally lowered his sword and thrust it back into its sheath.

"I think it's gone," he said as he looked down the river. "You can sit back up on the bench now, Clara."

Clara pulled herself up from the floor of the boat and sat back on the front bench. "Do you know what it was?"

"I'm not sure. I'm not aware of any large animals or fish in this river. Maybe—well, uhm, I'm not really sure. But it's gone now." Prince Dustin sat back down on the bench. He grabbed both oars and looked cautiously into the river as he pulled them through the water.

Both Clara and Prince Dustin remained silent. The only noise they heard coming from the river was the soft splash of the water as Prince Dustin rowed their small boat. Clara continued to hear the hoot owls in the distance, and every once in a while, she heard the crying sound of a baby. She was now less afraid of the animals that made those sounds.

Prince Dustin kept rowing, however, his pace got slower and slower. After rowing for a while his breathing started to become erratic, no longer in rhythm with each sweep of the oars. He was still weak. Clara looked up into the night sky and wondered what time it was. How long had they been traveling down the river? Surely it had to have been at least a couple of hours since they'd left her parlor. However, time seemed different here in the Black Forest. The sky was still black, and morning seemed to be a long way off.

"Clara," said Prince Dustin, "you may want to rest. We still have a way to go before we reach the borders of Queen Nordika's kingdom in the Land of Snow. I'm going to rest, too. The current is picking up, and it can carry us down the river."

Both Clara and Prince Dustin sat on the floor of the boat and rested their heads on the benches. The boat rocked back and forth as it traveled downstream, pushed by the current. Within minutes, Clara was sound asleep.

Clara dreamt about the Christmas Eve party and her Nutcracker Prince. She dreamt about Fritz and his friends and how they tossed her Nutcracker Prince doll around the parlor. She then saw her mom and dad. Clara dreamt it was Christmas morning and they were opening presents.

She dreamt about her Uncle Drosselmeyer. However, in her dream, he wore a wizard cap instead of his rumpled top hat. She dreamt about everyone laughing and dancing and having a great time at the party.

The current of the river quickened as Clara and Prince Dustin slept. The river was taking them downstream at a very fast pace. The movement of the boat rocked them further and further into sleep until it lulled them into a drunken stupor. Neither Prince Dustin nor Clara was aware of their surroundings, they were now characters in their own dreams.

The deep forest and evergreens were replaced by a mountain. The river continued and wrapped around the side of the mountain. Over the years, erosion had created the step the river now drifted down. Their boat drifted past several small waterfalls that had been created by erosion. Their boat continued and continued. Although Prince Dustin had traveled down this channel before, a small earthquake had changed the mountain since then. Prince Dustin, still deep in sleep, was unaware of the mountain's changes.

The river got choppy as Prince Dustin and Clara slept. It whipped the small boat from side to side as it traveled down the side of the mountain. The sounds of the forest were replaced by the sounds of the river as it broke against the mountainside. The terrain that grew in the crevices of the step of the mountainside kept the boat from slamming into the mountain's wall.

As the river's current quickened, Clara's dreams turned black. Her fairy tales turned into nightmares. She dreamt she was alone and running through a forest. Something was chasing her. Then she was no longer in the forest. She dreamt about the loud sounds coming out of the parlor. She dreamt about skittering noises and the sound of claws scratching the floorboards.

In her dream, it sounded like Fritz's pet mouse was running across the floor, but the *screeching-scratching-skittering* sounds were much louder than a small mouse could make. She had lit a candle that was on her bedside table to light her way. She dreamt about walking down the steps and wanting to turn around at every step but couldn't. She dreamt about something calling her into the grand parlor.

Her dreams took her back to her parlor. She dreamt about her Nutcracker Prince doll coming to life, a real prince, and his soldiers, all dutiful and skilled, protecting their prince from *them.*

She didn't see *them* at first, she just felt them. She was being watched. One by one *they* came. They taunted her. The creatures of the night: large mice, with incisors that seemed so sharp she could only imagine the prey that was at the mercy of those scissor sharp teeth. Their tails, quick and fast, hurling and hurling and hurling all around. Their leader looked even more *sinister.* His stare had brought chills to

Clara's bones. And it stared at her, for what seemed like hours.

SWISH-SWOOSH SWISH-SWOOSH SWISH-SWOOSH!

The river was getting even more violent, the boat holding Prince Dustin and Clara was no longer drifting but careening downstream. Prince Dustin was in a deep sleep, he didn't seem to be dreaming at all. His body was completely limp as he slept in harmony with the motion of the river. Clara's eyelids, however, were vibrating. Her eyes were moving rapidly back and forth as her nightmare continued.

Clara dreamt...why were the creatures in her parlor? Why were they attacking her? Why were they after her Nutcracker Prince? *They* were all around her, gnawing, gnawing, gnawing with those sharp teeth and whipping their long tails.

Prince Dustin and Clara continued to sleep as their boat was fast approaching a whirlpool that had formed in the river. The whirlpool was spinning, spitting out small rocks that had fallen from the side of the mountain and tossing them into a gushing waterfall, out of sight.

The waterfall was magnificent and beautiful, about twenty-five feet wide, with a drop several times that deep. The water was rushing down from the mountain's ledge, creating frothy bubbles—foamy white, light and airy. The bubbles were playful, a striking contrast to the violence of the water plunging and striking as it cascaded down the side of the mountain. As with many of Mother Nature's creations, the more beautiful, the more deadly, and the waterfall ahead was no exception.

The back and forth motion of the boat finally awakened Prince Dustin. It took him only moments to assess the danger upon them. He glared at the cyclone movement of the whirlpool ahead as it flung objects down the waterfall. He knew their boat was just moments away from being caught in the eye of the whirlpool.

Prince Dustin jumped up on his knees, almost falling out the boat and screamed, "Clara! Wake up! Clara, Clara! Wake up!" as he shook her vigorously.

Clara, startled by Prince Dustin, hit her head on the wall of the rowboat. Touching her head where it had been hit, she sensed trouble and quickly turned in the direction Prince Dustin was pointing. The fierce current of the whirlpool was swirling, pulling them into its grip.

SWOOSH! SWOOSH! SWOOSH!

Prince Dustin desperately looked for a way to escape the whirlpool.

SWOOSH! SWOOSH! SWOOSH!

He stood up in the boat, readying himself to fly. His body did not rise, he was still too weak to fly.

SWOOSH! SWOOSH! SWOOSH!

He looked to the sides of the river. The whirlpool took up the entire width of the river, so they couldn't get around it.

SWOOSH! SWOOSH! SWOOSH!

Prince Dustin looked up the side of the mountain, maybe thinking they could jump out of the boat and climb up the mountain's side. However, the wall of the mountain was slick and smooth.

SWOOSH! SWOOSH!! SWOOSH!

Clara's thoughts were racing. Their small rowboat was veering closer and closer to the whipping, swirling water of the whirlpool. Clara hopelessly looked to the floor of the boat, hoping to find something that could help them. She already knew, however, that nothing was lying on the floor of the boat.

Water was now getting inside their small rowboat and splashing all around them. They were soaked. The water kept coming for them.

SWOOSH! SWOOSH! SWOOSH!

Prince Dustin looked around frantically and finally exclaimed, "Clara, we are going to hit the whirlpool and go over the waterfall!"

Clara just kept looking at the whipping-whirling-whirlpool pulling them closer and closer. She was terrified. She wanted to be brave for Prince Dustin but had never been more frightened.

Prince Dustin shouted, "Clara, get down on the floor and wrap your arms around the bench! Don't let go no matter what!"

Clara tried to pretend she wasn't afraid, but she was trembling in terror. The whirlpool was sucking them in and was going to toss them to their doom.

Water had entirely flooded the bottom of their boat. They held on tightly to the wooden benches. Clara closed her eyes. She hoped she was still dreaming. Even her nightmares were better than this horror.

SWOOOOOOOOOSH!

DEEP IN THE BLACK FOREST

The rowboat was swept into the whirlpool!

-10-

Egon

"Your Highness." The lieutenant bowed as he greeted Egon.

Egon narrowed his already squinty black beady eyes and with a low gruff voice hissed back, "And who gave you permission to speak?"

The lieutenant trembled fiercely and fell down to his knees. He kept his head bowed. "Uh, sir, uh uh–"

"You blubbering piece of humanoid, can't you talk?" Egon growled as he slowly pulled his sword from its holster. He always kept his sword accessible. It was made of the purest silver and was sharpened twice a day. It could slice through anything like a knife through butter. Egon was always amused when he cut off the tail of a "despicable" mouse. When bored, he would have a poor mouse creature brought to his chamber and slash his sword several times, chopping off the poor mouse's tail, bit by bit, until only a stump was left.

"Your Highness of the Highest High, I beg you to forgive me for I know not what I speak and am unworthy to address thee!" the lieutenant squealed, begging for mercy.

Egon cocked his head and lowered his shoulders. "And what news do you have?"

"Wuh, uh, uhm—"

Egon grabbed the handle of his sword as the lieutenant fumbled over his words.

The lieutenant quickly composed himself and continued, "Yes, Your Highness. I have news of your brother and Prince Dustin."

Still on his knees, the lieutenant saw the glint of silver as Egon grabbed the handle of his sword again and started pulling it back out of its holster. "I mean *Dustin!*" the lieutenant screamed apologetically, not saying *Prince* this time.

Egon blinked both his beady eyes once and lowered his sword back into its holster. He looked down at the trembling lieutenant and kicked him in the butt. The lieutenant fell forward, flat on his face. His snout turned purple from being slammed on the hard concrete.

"Are you speaking to the floor? Stand," Egon ordered with a smirk. "How do you expect me to hear you from down there?"

The lieutenant quickly jumped up. His knees were knocking. With his head bowed and eyes lowered, the lieutenant acknowledged Egon with an anxious nod.

"You may proceed," Egon said. He had become bored with the "trifling" lieutenant and was ready to hear about the attack against Dustin. "And that pitiful excuse for a wizard thought he would fool us by turning Dustin into a Nutcracker doll." Egon cackled. He then swished the mucus around in his mouth and sharply spat. The lieutenant looked from the corners of his lowered eyes at the thick greenish-yellow spit on the gray concrete floor.

With a look of trepidation, the lieutenant reported to Egon, telling him how the Mouse King was slain by Dustin. The lieutenant also disclosed how the Mouse King was about to slay Dustin but was distracted by a young girl chosen by Drosselmeyer to protect Dustin as the Nutcracker Prince doll.

Egon, although younger than his brother, was much stronger and much more ruthless. Many in the kingdom thought the Mouse King was level-headed compared to his younger brother, Egon. The Mouse King was more strategic in his attacks, while Egon would pick fights for no reason. He was the strongest and best-skilled fighter in the Kingdom of Bosartig and would challenge anyone who appeared to be a threat, always to their demise.

As the lieutenant continued, Egon became visibly more and more vehement. His eyes, a pool of the blackest of black, began to form rings of red around them. His whiskers, so sharp that their tips could puncture flesh, were pointed straight out, off the sides of his face. His cheeks hollowed. His face no longer looked like that of a mouse but of a rat. The more the lieutenant shared about the battle, the angrier Egon became, physically changing as he got madder and madder.

The lieutenant stepped back as he continued to tell the events of the battle.

Egon's nostrils fumed smoke as the lieutenant spoke, not circles of smoke puffs, but a grayish white cloud of smoke was thundering from his nostrils. As the lieutenant spoke, Egon rapidly gnawed on his front incisors, his teeth became sharper, more pointed, and whiter the more he gnawed. They were now glistening white. Egon grimaced and pulled back his lips, exposing his gums, the smoke fumes had turned his gums from soft pink to black.

The lieutenant said sheepishly as he bowed with his knees knocking, "Your Highness, you are now King of Bosartig."

❖ ❖ ❖

In the Land of Snow, Queen Nordika received news from Drosselmeyer that the Mouse King had been slain by Prince Dustin. He also relayed to her that Prince Dustin was bringing the young girl, Clara, with him to protect the girl from Egon. He informed Queen Nordika that Prince Dustin would be weak from his transition back to a human prince.

Queen Nordika summoned the assistance of Bronson the Beaver of the River Country. She told the beaver about the battle between Prince Dustin and the Mouse King. She also told him how Prince Dustin had been turned into a Nutcracker Prince doll by

Drosselmeyer to protect Prince Dustin and his kingdom from attacks by the Mouse King.

Everyone in the Black Forest knew Prince Dustin would become King of Konfetenburg on his fifteenth birthday. Once king, Prince Dustin would have all the armies of the nearby kingdoms in the Black Forest at his full disposal.

Bronson the Beaver was well aware of the importance of Prince Dustin becoming King of Konfetenburg and the impact it would have on the balance of power in the Black Forest. The kingdoms would then be impregnable to attacks by Egon and the Kingdom of Bosartig.

The beavers considered themselves neutral, being creatures of land and water. They never took part in the battles that took place on land in the Black Forest. However, the beavers did understand that peace on the land impacted life on the river. Queen Nordika could always count on them to secretly support her crusades. It helped both the beavers and Queen Nordika to keep their alliance private.

For centuries, the King of the Land of Konfetenburg had kept peace throughout all the kingdoms, until the Mouse King's father died and the Mouse King became King. The Mouse King, in his pursuit of power, started attacking weaker kingdoms. Now that Egon was king of the mouse people, it was expected that the attacks on the kingdoms would be even more frequent and severe.

Queen Nordika called upon Bronson to bring Prince Dustin and Clara quickly to her kingdom in the Land of

Snow. She knew the quickest path was through the tunnels in the caves. Bronson could guide them to the Land of Snow in a little over an hour and save Prince Dustin and Clara from what could otherwise be a two to three days' journey under good conditions.

❖ ❖ ❖

After speaking with Queen Nordika, Bronson the Beaver swiftly left the Ice Palace to find Prince Dustin and the young girl, Clara. Time was not on his side, Egon, now King Egon, would be hot on their trail. If King Egon reached Prince Dustin before Bronson, Bronson knew there would be little hope for Clara or Prince Dustin.

❖ ❖ ❖

Egon, spewing and cursing, trampled through the halls of the Castle of Bosartig. He was rage walking. All the mice in the kingdom that saw him from a distance backed off and quickly fled the other way, probably hoping they had not been spotted. Those less fortunate, quickly learned the folly of being in the path of a mouse gone mad.

Egon had already given orders to have all the mouse soldiers ready by the time he made it to the front of the castle.

The mouse soldiers were lined up row by row by the time Egon made it out to the castle's courtyard. Many gulped when Egon appeared.

"Mice!" Egon bellowed.

"Yes, King Egon." The mouse soldiers shivered as they quickly knelt in unison.

King Egon thrust his sword in the air above his head. "We are on our way to the Ice Palace. Nordika thinks her army can protect Dustin and that young girl. Can she protect them?" Egon said with an evil laugh.

The mouse soldiers said nothing. They hung their heads low.

"You!" Egon hollered as he pointed to one of the mouse soldiers up front. All heads immediately turned. Some mice could be heard sighing with relief. Egon was not speaking to them.

The soldier Egon pointed out quickly ran forward. Directly in front of Egon, he knelt down on one knee and bowed his head. "Yes, King Egon," he said meekly, almost in a whisper. Tears could be seen welling up in the soldier's eyes.

"I remember you from our last battle," Egon continued as he walked from side to side with his head held high.

The poor mouse soldier softly responded, "Yes."

"Stand and look behind you!" Egon ordered while he rammed his sword into its holster.

The mouse soldier jumped up and looked at the rows of mouse soldiers still kneeling with their faces partly lowered.

"Now, tell me what you see."

The mouse soldier looked perplexed and gulped. In a shrill and confused voice, he responded, "Mouse soldiers?"

Egon walked from left to right and templed his sharp claws, tapping them together in front of his chest. "Yes, mouse soldiers," he affirmed in a commanding low voice. "And none of those faces will be here tomorrow if we don't get that girl and Dustin by the stroke of the next hour."

Egon then charged forward. The mouse soldiers followed quickly behind him. Their long tails swished from side to side, leaving marks in the snow.

◆ ◆ ◆

SWOOSH! SWOOSH! SWOOSH!

Clara closed her eyes and held on tight as their small boat was swept into the whirlpool. Her heart was pounding so hard she couldn't differentiate between the pounding of her heart and the swirling, pounding movement of the whirlpool. The whirlpool was whipping their boat all around, teasing them, taking its time before tossing them down the throat of the waterfall into the jagged rocks below. Prince Dustin and Clara were soaked. The water beat them with every twist. Clara felt like she was drowning from the water pounding against her face.

SWOOSH! SWOOSH! SWOOSH!

Then it happened. Clara felt their boat slowly tipping, tipping, t-i-p-p-i-n-g over the ledge of the waterfall, not a fast jerk, but very slowly it tipped their boat as if it was changing its mind midway, as if the whirlpool wanted them to feel her wrath, as if it wanted them to feel doom.

"Little girl, didn't your mother ever tell you to respect Mother Nature?" the whirlpool seemed to say. When the whirlpool seemed to be done playing with them, it tossed them down the gushing waterfall.

Clara felt their boat rushing down the throat of the waterfall. For a moment, she was relieved to no longer be tossed around in the whirlpool. She wanted to open her eyes. She wanted to make sure her Nutcracker Prince had not fallen out of the boat. She knew she had to be strong, she had to open her eyes. Her Nutcracker Prince might need her, and she wanted to be there for him.

Clara opened her eyes and saw Prince Dustin, her Nutcracker Prince. He was watching her like a protective brother. He smiled at her. It was only a brief moment but felt like an eternity. Clara smiled back at her Nutcracker Prince. A moment later, Prince Dustin watched as Clara's smiling face was replaced by horror seen in her eyes.

The bench had come loose. The side of the bench Clara was clutching broke from the wall of the boat. Her fleeting moment of hope was quickly dashed. She blinked at Prince Dustin one last time.

"Clara!" Prince Dustin screamed as he watched Clara fall out of the boat.

Before he could jump in behind her, the waterfall jerked the boat, pulling him back into its grips. The small boat, with Prince Dustin still in it, hit the water below. Within moments, Prince Dustin was riding the currents down the river.

Clara was gone.

·11·

Overboard

Egon is coming! Bronson moved swiftly. *I have to get to them first, or –.*

"Prince Dustin would not have regained his strength. He will most probably be coming to the Ice Palace with Clara." Bronson kept remembering the words of Queen Nordika as he trekked quickly through the forest. He had to get to the Great Waterfall.

"Egon will have no mercy." Bronson mourned.

Bronson the Beaver didn't want to belabor what would happen if Egon found Prince Dustin and the young girl before he did. He knew his mission was dire. Bronson made it to the river as fast as he could. His webbed feet made it easier for him to travel in the snow. He skated most of the way.

Bronson heard the cries of the bobcats in the distance. He had never been fond of them. *I wouldn't mind them so much if they didn't cry throughout the night,* he thought. It really annoyed him.

The owls were everywhere tonight, Bronson noticed. He remembered one of the younger beavers saying, "Yeah, they're smart, I'll give them that—just nosy—always turning their heads around so they don't miss nothin'." Bronson grinned, remembering.

Ah uuuuuuuuuh! Ah uuuuuuuuuh! Ah uuuuuuuuuh!

Bronson's mood changed quickly. He heard howling coming from the distance. The wolves were friends of no one—animal or man. They roamed the Black Forest at night hunting for prey. Hunting was a game the wolves played. Each night they would hunt in packs and identify a target. The wolf that slaughtered their target was declared the winner of the nightly hunt. *I hope Prince Dustin and Clara are not their targets tonight,* Bronson sighed.

Bronson had already sent word to the beaver scouts that lived in the River Country to locate Prince Dustin and a young girl, "Inform all of the scouts that they are needed stat!" Bronson had ordered. "Prince Dustin and the young girl will be traveling down the river to the Ice Palace. We need to find them."

"Egon will seek revenge and they are in danger. Especially the young girl, Clara" Queen Nordika had told Bronson. Bronson moved faster as he thought about the Snow Queen's remarks.

Bronson knew he had to find Prince Dustin before Egon, now King Egon. Without Prince Dustin and his army, the kingdoms in the Black Forest would be powerless against Egon. It was believed, and rightly so, that Egon would waste no time in attacking the kingdoms in the Black Forest. It would be brutal. All would be killed, captured, or worse.

❖ ❖ ❖

Earlier in the night, Prince Dustin and Clara were spotted, almost immediately, after they landed in the Black Forest. Bryon the Beaver was the first to see them. He was at his station and saw two figures glide through the sky. They landed at the bank of the River Stromabwarts.

As Prince Dustin and Clara walked down the river's path, Bryon swam alongside them in the river. He avoided being seen. He was not in range of the next beaver colony and would have to wait until he was in range to send a message.

Beavers slapped their tails to send messages. The beavers' tails were so wide and flat that birds and small animals that happened to be close would be quite startled when the beavers slapped their tails.

When in range, Bryon would be able to slap his large wide tail in the river to send a message to the next scout, informing the scout that he had spotted Prince Dustin and Clara. The next beaver scout would then take charge and immediately send a message. This chain of communication would continue until the message reached Bronson.

All the beaver scouts were pals. Bryon was particularly fond of Trudy. Trudy was a girl scout in the next colony. Once Prince Dustin and Clara walked down the river's bank and got to the area called, *The*

Resting Site, Bryon would be within range and could then send a message to Trudy.

The area was called, *The Resting Site,* because people and others who inhabited the Black Forest often rested on the tree stumps that remained. The trees had been chopped down long, long ago.

Prince Dustin and Clara were now at The Resting Site. They had stopped to rest on the tree stumps. All the beaver colonies were now within range of the next colony. Messages could now be communicated down the river within minutes, eventually reaching Bronson at the Great Waterfall.

Bryon was so excited. He could finally signal Trudy and slap his tail. He splashed and splashed and then slapped his tail several times in the river.

SLAP SLAP SLAP SLAP SLAP SLAP SLAP SLAP SLAP!

"We have to leave *now!*" Bryon heard Prince Dustin exclaim. Bryon might have slapped his tail too hard. He probably frightened Prince Dustin and Clara, he thought. Prince Dustin immediately grabbed the handle of his sword. Clara was obviously frightened. Bryon noticed that Clara looked at the river anxiously. Her eyes were wide with fear. Bryon then bowed his head sheepishly and submerged himself fully underwater. He felt bad that he had startled Clara.

❖ ❖ ❖

Trudy felt the wave caused by the slapping of Bryon's tail. Trudy, although the only girl beaver scout, was considered one of the best scouts in the River Country. "That must be Bryon!" she acknowledged silently. *Prince Dustin and the young girl, Clara, must be traveling down the river and be in my area now.*

SLAP SLAP SLAP!

Trudy slapped her tail and sent a message to the beaver scout in the next colony. Soon the message reached Bronson that Prince Dustin and Clara were traveling down the river toward the Great Waterfall.

❖ ❖ ❖

Whew! They are safe, Bronson thought when he got the message. It was also reported that one of the scouts got too close and collided into the bottom of Prince Dustin and Clara's small boat, almost toppling it over. Bronson shook his head— *Bryon, I'm sure. He is always so clumsy.*

Bronson was ready to meet Prince Dustin and Clara at the Great Waterfall and guide them through the caves to Queen Nordika's Ice Palace. He had decided to wait at the bottom of the waterfall, where the river wrapped around the mountain and continued downstream.

He would inform Prince Dustin that Queen Nordika charged him with navigating them through the tunnels and caves of the Black Forest. They would be able to get to the Land of Snow quickly by going through the caves—before Egon caught up to them. Bronson also knew that until Prince Dustin regained his full strength, the Black Forest was a treacherous place for both the Prince and the young girl, Clara.

❖ ❖ ❖

I'm falling! Clara grabbed at the water. With her eyes partly closed, she could only see white foam. She opened her mouth to scream. Water swished in then out her mouth.

The bench that Clara had been gripping became dislodged from the wall of the boat. Clara tried to reach out for Prince Dustin's hand. Everything happened so quickly! Clara thought she was dreaming. She closed her eyes to keep water from getting in them.

Clara wanted to open her eyes, but kept them closed. Everything that had happened, since she had gone to bed, suddenly flashed through her mind. She wanted it to be morning. She wanted to see Fritz jumping on her bed like he always did every Christmas.

Clara felt herself fall out of the boat and was plummeting down the waterfall! It was not a dream, not even a nightmare. *This is really happening,* Clara thought bleakly.

"Hah hah hah, little girl." Clara thought she heard the waterfall laugh. "Who gave you permission to ride my fall?"

Clara exclaimed, "I'm sorry!"

"Too late! The deed has already been done—hah hah hah! Hah hah hah!" Clara heard as she was pushed down the throat of the Great Waterfall.

◆ ◆ ◆

Bronson was waiting at the bottom of the Great Waterfall. He did not see any signs of the small boat with Prince Dustin and Clara. The stars lit the sky like flecks of white paint on a black velvet canvas. He knew Prince Dustin and Clara would be arriving at this point in the river soon. Bronson had always loved this spot. On a sunny day, a rainbow of colors from red to gold to indigo blue would stretch across the horizon directly above the waterfall.

It was night. The Great Waterfall's magnificence could be seen from a far distance. Every night the moon revolved on its axis to showcase different works created by Mother Nature. It reminded Bronson that all creatures, no matter how great, were insignificant in comparison.

Bronson looked up at the top of the waterfall. He gazed at the water cascading down. The water was beating against the side of the mountain. He thought about how the pounding of the water would feel on his back. Many times he would come to the waterfall for a massage. The pounding of the water was so relaxing. Tonight he had important business. He would have to wait until next time, he mulled.

What's that? Looking up at the top of the waterfall, Bronson thought he saw the helm of a small boat. Yes, it was a boat. *It must be Prince Dustin and Clara*, he thought. Bronson's smile quickly turned into a frown. A violent whirlpool of water was tossing the small boat all around.

Bronson panicked. The beautiful waterfall that Bronson had seen earlier now looked like a torturous machine, whipping and thrashing the small boat. It would only be a matter of moments before the boat was hurled into the river below. Bronson knew he had to act fast.

They are going overboard! Prince Dustin can swim. I don't know about Clara, Bronson thought grimly. He looked at the river's current. At the speed it was moving, it would pull Clara downstream before he got to her.

Bronson vaulted into the icy river water. He was a fast swimmer. Beavers used their webbed feet and swam like fish. Because of Bronson's size, the current had little impact on him. If Clara survived the waterfall, he wanted to be able to pull her out quickly before the current carried her downstream. The moon was still lighting the waterfall and the river below. *I must hurry!* Bronson had no time to spare.

Bronson looked up. The small boat was now teetering at the top of the waterfall. Then it happened– the small boat plunged down the waterfall.

Bronson saw Clara. She fell overboard. He saw her struggling to grab at something, but there was nothing to grab. Her hands just slipped through the water. Bronson swam faster toward the bottom of the waterfall.

SPLASH!

Bronson felt the water ripple as Clara splashed hard into the river. He saw her immediately. She was not too far from him.

Bronson grabbed Clara by her shoulders. Her eyes were closed tight. He felt her heart pounding. Bronson kept her head above the water as he swam as fast as he could. The river's current kept trying to grab Clara out of his arms, but Bronson held onto Clara tightly.

❖ ❖ ❖

Clara kept her eyes closed tight as she was carried out of the river. She knew how to swim, but wasn't sure, how she would do, under these conditions. It all had happened so quickly. Clara was surprised that Prince Dustin was able to rescue her—*My Nutcracker Prince*, Clara thought. She was glad Prince Dustin had been able to jump in after her, after all.

❖ ❖ ❖

Bronson laid Clara down on the terrain at the bank of the river. Her eyes were still closed. Bronson hovered over Clara, looking for signs that she was still breathing. Clara's chest was moving up and down. Bronson moved closer. His face was right above Clara's.

Then—Clara opened her eyes.

"Aghhh!" Clara screamed.

Bronson was startled. He jumped up and fell back on his butt. Bronson's fur was soaking wet. His claws were protruding out from his webbed feet.

Clara gawked at Bronson. She then passed out.

-12-

Creatures of the Night

Prince Dustin had moved to Clara's side of the boat as quickly as he could. He desperately extended his arms and tried to catch Clara.

"Clara!" Prince Dustin shouted as he watched Clara fall out of the boat.

Prince Dustin panted. If he had only been a little closer to Clara, he could have caught her before she fell, he thought. Everything had happened so quickly that by the time he realized Clara was falling, it was too late. Prince Dustin peered over the side of the boat.

"Clara, I'm coming for you!" The sound of Prince Dustin's voice was lost in the thundering waterfall.

Prince Dustin strained to see Clara through the waterfall's thick foam. He saw her hit the river. Prince Dustin pulled himself up to jump in after Clara, but the force of the water jerked the small boat and knocked him back down. The small boat then crashed into the river.

The current swiftly carried the small boat downstream before Prince Dustin could regain his footing. He anxiously looked back, searching for Clara. Out of the corner of his eye, he saw something pulling Clara out of the water. *It* was carrying her toward the river's bank. Prince Dustin could not see *it* clearly. Whatever *it* was, *it* had Clara.

Egon has Clara! Prince Dustin feared. He quickly reasoned that whatever it was that had Clara, it was too dark to be Egon. Prince Dustin was somewhat relieved but still worried.

One of the oars was lodged under the bench and did not go overboard. Prince Dustin used it to row the small boat to the side of the river. The river's bank was mostly clear of trees, and there was a slight path leading back toward the waterfall. *That path will lead me to Clara.*

Prince Dustin made it to the shore and jumped out of the boat. He pulled the boat far out of the water. He didn't waste any time. *I have to get to Clara* was all he could think about. His uniform was soaked. It turned a darker shade of red and blue. His hair was drenching wet, and his eyelashes held beads of water as the water dripped down from his hair to his forehead. Prince Dustin shook his head and the water splattered.

Prince Dustin charged down the path as quickly as he could. The path was clear of snow, so he was able to get a good foothold. He knew he had to find Clara before she was taken too far away from the waterfall. *I have to hurry or I may never see her again, like my parents.* He felt that he was slowly getting his strength back. He was actually moving at a fast pace, much faster than he thought he would be able to do. He knew he would have to go into the forest to find Clara. He just hoped he had the strength to overpower whatever it was that had taken her.

The moon was lighting Prince Dustin's path back to the waterfall. Beyond the trees, in the forest, it was pitch black. The evergreen trees were so thick Prince Dustin knew he would not be able to maneuver as quickly.

I hope I find Clara before that creature drags her through the forest! He thought that if he moved quickly, he could surprise the creature, catch it off guard and rescue Clara.

Prince Dustin knew he had an even bigger worry. *Egon!* If Egon found Clara before he did, then there would be no hope for her.

❖ ❖ ❖

"We must prepare for battle!" Queen Nordika announced.

Except for the Kingdom of Konfetenburg, Queen Nordika had the largest army in the Black Forest. Her soldiers were fierce and relentless. She used her army to keep peace and only deployed them when peace throughout the Black Forest was in jeopardy.

"Prince Dustin and Clara will be here soon. I need you to give orders to the soldiers that they need to be ready within an hour," Queen Nordika said to the head of her army.

◆ ◆ ◆

Prince Dustin moved more slowly as he approached the waterfall. He didn't want to alert the creature that had taken Clara. The Great Waterfall was just ahead. Drops from the cascading water were hitting his face. Prince Dustin didn't seem to notice. He had just a short stretch to go to make it back to the place where Clara had been pulled out of the river. He wished he could tell Clara, "Be brave, I'm coming for you."

Prince Dustin thought about the creature that took Clara. The Black Forest was full of creatures big and small. Some of the creatures had four legs, and some with even more. The deeper one went inside the Black Forest, the stranger the creatures.

Prince Dustin remembered stories he had been told since he was young about one of the creatures deep in the Black Forest. "They have no name, they are simply called *Kreaturs*. They roam only at night and prey upon whatever crosses their path. The male kills all male *Kreaturs* that are born. Only the females are allowed to live. The females are as vicious as the male."

"Once the male is old, he allows a male to survive and grooms him to take over the clan. *Kreaturs* have a face that resembles a grizzly, with razor-sharp teeth. Their body is muscular like that of a cheetah, only they have six legs. *Kreaturs* have short, coarse fur coats that are a blend of black, gray, and brown stripes. Their tail is long, lithe, and spiked at the tip."

Prince Dustin remembered that *Kreaturs* lived very deep inside the Black Forest and were *rarely seen elsewhere*. They lived so deeply inside the Black Forest that Prince Dustin had never heard of anyone who had journeyed that far. He now was worried about what was meant by *rarely seen elsewhere.*

Prince Dustin shuddered as he remembered the tales he had been told. "If you see a *Kreatur*, hide! You cannot outrun them. You cannot outfight them. You will not survive them. Hide!"

Prince Dustin felt confident that a *Kreatur* did not have Clara. *At least I hope not.* He finally made it back to the place where Clara had been taken. Drawing his sword from its sheath, Prince Dustin got ready to attack the creature that had taken Clara. He raised his sword with great force.

With his sword held high, Prince Dustin was ready to defend Clara. He looked all around. He didn't want to be caught off guard by a surprise attack. The stars were still bright and shining down from above. However, Prince Dustin did not see a creature.

The creature was gone. Clara was gone, too. Prince Dustin sullenly looked for traces of the creature. Then he saw something!

On the ground—next to a tree, Prince Dustin saw a green hair ribbon. It was Clara's bow. It was just a few feet away from where he was standing, behind a huge evergreen tree. The tree was so big Prince Dustin couldn't see behind it.

Prince Dustin then spotted them behind the tree. *They're behind that tree.* The creature was hiding Clara. Prince Dustin panted fiercely as he thrust his sword forward. He moved lightly and slowly toward the tree. He didn't know what creature it was, but he was sure it wasn't a *Kreatur*. A *Kreatur* would have attacked him by now.

With each step, Prince Dustin clenched his sword tighter and moved forward slowly, keenly narrowing his eyes, sharpening his view.

Prince Dustin was close to the tree now. As the best marksman in the Black Forest, Prince Dustin knew speed was how to gain an advantage over an opponent. He spun around the tree quickly, pulled his elbow back and lunged.

However, Clara was not there. No Clara. No creature. It was just a fallen tree branch.

Prince Dustin looked down at the soft snow. He saw footprints! One set was Clara's. The other prints were of a very large animal, maybe the size of a bear. He knew that from the shape of the prints, they were not prints of a bear. Prince Dustin pondered, *Could these be the prints of a...* He shook his head and shrugged it off without finishing his thought. The prints were much too large to be from the animal that came to his mind.

Prince Dustin followed the footprints into the woods, leaving the moonlit glow of the river. In the forest, the moon peeked through the treetops just enough for him to be able to follow the footprints. He thought how frightened Clara must be, and quickened his pace. Prince Dustin weaved in and out between the trees.

He stopped at a small clearing in the woods. *Something's watching me.* Prince Dustin slowly looked all around and gripped his sword tighter, but he didn't see anything.

DEEP IN THE BLACK FOREST

He looked down at the snow for prints. He no longer saw two sets of prints, only the prints of the creature. He shuddered at the thought. *What happened to Clara?* Prince Dustin knew he had to hurry to save Clara if it wasn't already too late.

He looked all around, he still didn't see anything. He was sure that he was being watched. He moved past the clearing and darted back into the wooded area of the forest. After going a short distance, he heard the sounds of animals. He stopped in his tracks and listened.

Ah uuuuuuuuuuh! Ah uuuuuuuuuuh! Ah uuuuuuuuuuh!

One after another, the wolves howled a deep, throaty cry. The wolves were communicating. The cries started off low but got more piercing before winding down. They were definitely communicating, but what? One after another they howled. Prince Dustin knew he had to move quickly to avoid being in the middle of the pack.

The gray wolves that lived in the Black Forest were much fiercer and more territorial. They attacked anything that wandered into their territory. Smelling the scent of the wolves, most of the animals of the Black Forest stayed away from the wolves' territory.

The creature that had Clara was obviously not afraid of the wolves. It took Clara through the wolves' territory. Although, from the marks of the prints, it was obvious to Prince Dustin that the creature was moving much faster.

The wolves' howls were getting closer. Prince Dustin was being hunted. He was the prey for the wolves' nightly game of hunt. Prince Dustin tried to lift himself up. He tried to fly. Unfortunately, he was unable to lift his body off the ground. He was still too weak to fly.

Prince Dustin knew the wolves would eventually catch up to him. He also knew he could not stop, in hopes that they would pass him. He had to keep following the tracks of the creature that had Clara.

WOOF- WOOF- WOOF- WOOF- WOOF-WOOF!

The wolves were no longer howling, they were barking. The wolves had closed the distance between themselves and Prince Dustin. They no longer had to howl to communicate. They were now a pack!

-13-

The Cave

Why did it bring me here? Clara wondered. *It doesn't seem to want to hurt me.*

Clara said softly, "Mr. uh, Bear? Uh, Mr. uh, Animal?" Clara was not sure what kind of animal it was.

The animal looked at Clara with gentle eyes.

Clara looked around at the gray and white coarse stone walls with splotches of copper and gold tones. She was surprised the air smelled fresh. She had never been inside a cave but would have it expected it to smell differently.

The animal and Clara were in the entrance chamber of the cave. The cave was dark but not pitch-black. Although dimly lit, it was actually lighter inside the cave than in the Black Forest. On the ground of the cave, crystals were casting off a soft golden glow, lighting the cave.

Clara cautiously picked up one of the crystals, expecting it to be warm, but it was cool to her touch. She examined it carefully. She remembered seeing a stone like it before. Clara reached inside the top of her gown and pulled out the crystal necklace Prince Dustin had given her in her parlor. "This crystal will keep you warm deep in the Black Forest," Clara remembered her Nutcracker Prince saying.

"Prince Dustin gave me this one," Clara said to the animal, showing the animal her crystal necklace. She knew the animal didn't know what she was saying, but there was nobody else to talk to. "He said it would keep me warm. And I haven't felt cold at all," she continued.

The animal grunted something back at Clara. It sounded like a friendly grunt, Clara thought. She remembered her mother always said, "Kindness is a universal language." Clara then smiled back at the animal as she tucked the crystal necklace back underneath her gown. She looked back at the crystals glowing on the ground. She then looked underneath her gown. Her crystal glowed, too.

"Thank you for pulling me out of the river." Clara hoped the animal understood. The animal grunted another friendly-sounding grunt. Clara smiled. "I think you understand me," Clara said.

She looked at the random formations inside the cave. Clara observed that some formations hung like stone icicles, hanging down from the top of the cave. Others towered up from the ground like sculptures.

Clara also noticed that the ground she was sitting on was more like sand than dirt. It also had the same hues of color as the walls. Clara scraped at the stone wall behind her. The shavings fell to the ground and blended in with the sand. Clara had always been curious about things. However, she was usually too afraid to investigate her hunches.

CLAP-CLAP-CLAP-CLAP-CLAP-CLAP!

Clara jumped! Sounds were coming from a tunnel off the chamber. It led deeper into the cave. Clara wondered what could be lurking at the other end of the tunnel. She shivered at the thought. The sound of a streaming flow of water was also coming from the tunnel. If it were not for the clapping sound, the water would have sounded peaceful.

The clapping sound overlapped, as though several animals or creatures were making those sounds. "It sounds like lots of animals," Clara said aloud.

The animal grunted a deep gruff. Clara thought the animal's grunt this time was different. It was not friendly. It was as though the animal was also worried about the clapping sound. Clara wondered if he knew what animals were at the other end of the tunnel. The clapping sound continued. It did not stop.

CLAP-CLAP-CLAP-CLAP-CLAP-CLAP-CLAP-CLAP-CLAP-CLAP-CLAP-CLAP!

Clara looked over at the animal. She thought it looked like a beaver, just several times larger. She remembered seeing beavers when she visited her Uncle Drosselmeyer at his old mill. This animal was bigger than Clara. Much bigger than any beaver that Clara had ever seen. *It can't be a beaver, it's too big.*

Its fur was a deep chocolate brown and it had gentle black coal eyes. Clara was no longer afraid of the animal. She thought about how she would have drowned had it not pulled her out of the river. The animal seemed to be protecting her, Clara thought. At times, it was even trying to speak to her, although Clara didn't understand what it was saying. The animal also seemed to be taking her some place. Clara wondered, *Where?*

CLAP-CLAP-CLAP-CLAP-CLAP-CLAP   CLAP-CLAP-CLAP-CLAP-CLAP-CLAP!

The clapping continued. Clara thought back to when she fell overboard.

"Were you already in the river when you pulled me out?" Clara asked the animal. Before it could respond, Clara rattled a list of questions at the animal. She didn't expect the animal to understand. But again, nobody else was there to ask.

"There was someone with me in the boat when we fell down the waterfall. Did you see what happened to him? Did he fall out the boat, too? He lives here in the Black Forest. His name is Prince Dustin. Can you help me find him?"

The animal grunted several times.

Clara continued. "I'm not from here. I'm from a town outside the Black Forest. Prince Dustin said my Uncle Drosselmeyer is a wizard. Anyway, he turned Prince Dustin into a Nutcracker Prince doll—to hide him from the Mouse King." Clara noticed that the animal sat up attentively, and grunted from time to time as if it understood what she was saying.

"I was supposed to protect him as the Nutcracker Prince doll. Somehow the Mouse King found out." Clara's eyes were wide open and teary as she looked straight at the animal.

"My Nutcracker Prince doll turned into Prince Dustin." Clara was speaking fast now. "Then he was killed. Not Prince Dustin but the Mouse King."

"Then we had to leave because I guess he has a brother even more evil than him. Oh yes, his name is Egon." Clara noticed that the animal grunted roughly when she said Egon's name.

"He is after us!" Clara continued, panting as she spoke. "Was that howling we heard Egon?"

The animal grunted as though he was replying to Clara's question.

Clara thought back to when the animal pulled her out of the river. She and the animal had only been resting by the river for a short time when Clara heard howling coming out of the forest. It was at a distance, but the howling was coming from all directions. Although the sounds did not sound close, it still scared Clara. The animal seemed alarmed, too, Clara thought. After hearing the howling, the animal pulled her up, and they ran into the trees, into the darkness of the Black Forest.

Clara remembered looking up and not being able to see much of the moon or the stars. It was so dark. *And now it has me!* Clara remembered thinking. She was afraid of *it,* but even more afraid of the howling. *Egon found us*, she had thought.

Clara recalled that she and the animal continued running until they made it to a clearing in the forest. The light of the moon and stars comforted Clara at the time. She remembered being glad to be out of the woods. The howling had momentarily stopped but then started back. The animal even seemed alarmed. Its ears stood erect and its body stiffened, Clara remembered thinking.

After that, Clara recalled being startled by the bizarre actions of the animal that had pulled her out of the river and taken her into the forest. She didn't know what to think. She just watched. The animal knelt down and rubbed its paw briskly against the bottom bark of the closest tree.

Clara had wanted to run but was too afraid to move. The animal then rubbed whatever it took off the bark of the tree all over its furry coat, she recalled.

Clara remembered letting out a shriek of surprise as the animal swept her up in its large arms. It then dashed through the forest, back into the blackness of the evergreens. It skated on the snow. With its webbed feet, it was able to move extremely fast, Clara reflected.

It carried Clara all the rest of the way to the cave.

❖ ❖ ❖

Prince Dustin looked around. He knew he could not outrun the wolves. He was still weak. He also knew he could not fight them off, either. The mountain's side was directly ahead. It was steep, jagged, and almost entirely covered by shrubbery. Prince Dustin was still following the prints of the animal that had taken Clara. The prints led to the mountainside ahead. *It must have climbed up the mountain*, Prince Dustin thought as he charged forward.

It took only a few minutes for Prince Dustin to make it to the side of the mountain. He thought, *just in time*, as he heard rustling coming from the trees. *It must be the wolves!*

Prince Dustin then quickly grabbed a long vine that was hanging off the mountainside. Before pulling himself up onto the mountain with the vine, he looked back over his shoulder for the wolves.

However, he did not see the wolves. He also no longer heard their howling. What he did see was a very, very big, brown bear. The bear had found a small shrub, ripe with holly berries. It was taking its time, savoring every berry, as it ate them off the bush. Prince Dustin exhaled. The bear hadn't noticed him. Prince Dustin also knew that as long as the bear stayed there eating berries, he didn't have to worry about the wolves coming after him.

Prince Dustin turned and tugged at the vine on the mountainside. He lifted his foot to anchor it on the side of the mountain.

"Aaaaaaaaaaargh!" Instead of having a foothold on the side of the mountain, Prince Dustin fell with a thud into a cave. The cave's entrance was hidden behind all the shrubbery on the mountainside.

❖ ❖ ❖

Clara did not want to go down the passageway of the tunnel. *That's where the clapping sounds are coming from.* The animal that rescued her was pointing in that direction. It wanted to go through the tunnel. Clara was frightened. *Maybe it is not trying to protect me.*

Clara's heart was beating fast. She looked back at the shrubbery that covered the opening of the cave. She thought about the howling animals that were chasing after them. *Well, I don't want to go back into the Black Forest*, Clara thought.

She then looked down the dark tunnel. She still heard the clapping sounds. *Well, I don't really want to go that way either,* she sighed. She also reasoned that she did not want to hang around for Egon to find her.

Clara looked at the animal that had brought her to the cave. His eyes were gentle and she thought she could trust him. He definitely seemed to be protecting her from the dangers of the Black Forest. He also seemed to be on a mission. He seemed to want to get some place quickly. The animal grunted as if instructing Clara. Clara then followed the animal down the dark tunnel.

While walking through the tunnel, Clara thought about Prince Dustin. She hoped he was safe. She also thought about her brother, Fritz. It seemed like a long time ago when she was dancing at the Christmas party. She recalled being so excited at the time, that she didn't eat much at dinner. She wished she had some of Mrs. Koch's gingerbread cookies.

Clara wondered what time it was and suspected it was well into the night. If she were home, she knew she would be sound asleep, dreaming of the gifts and presents she would open on Christmas morning. Clara wished she were home, in her bed.

❖ ❖ ❖

Prince Dustin fell hard on his left side, the side where he kept his sword. The sword's leather sheath protected him from being cut. He got up and dusted the sand off his uniform. He knew there were many secret caves in the Black Forest. The mountains were mostly made of granite stone, so the caves were created over time by streams and corrosion. The caves were home to many creatures, some not seen for centuries outside the caves. The caves were very dangerous, and most people did not venture into them.

Prince Dustin had heard about the caves in the mountains that led to Queen Nordika's Ice Palace. He'd also heard that by going through the caves, a person could save a day or two in their journey to the Land of Snow. *I have to go through the caves, there's no other choice.* He had to get to the Ice Palace quickly. Maybe Queen Nordika could help him find Clara, he thought.

Prince Dustin listened. He heard the sound of a stream of water coming from a dark tunnel inside the cave. It sounded very distant, indicating the cave was very deep. He also heard an eerie clapping sound. He knew what was making that sound. He grimaced.

Just before he entered the dark tunnel, Prince Dustin noticed prints of the animal that had taken Clara. *The animal did not climb up the wall of the mountain after all. He came through the cave!*

Prince Dustin looked closer at the ground. Behind the animal's prints he saw Clara's footprints. Prince Dustin dashed through the tunnel after Clara.

-14-

Cave Creatures

Fresh meat! Bronson worried about Clara as they crept through the dark tunnel. He had traveled many times through the hidden caves and was well aware of the dangers ahead. He knew that the creatures would consider Clara, fresh meat.

However, it was a shortcut to get to Queen Nordika's Ice Palace, so he had to risk it. *They probably already smell us coming*, Bronson lamented quietly. His ears pricked as he keenly listened to the sounds coming out of the chamber ahead. Although the winged creatures had minimal vision, they could hear well and had a keen sense of smell.

Bronson was not worried about himself. Beavers were able to avoid the dangers of the winged creatures that lived inside the cave. Their thick fur coats protected them from attacks by the winged creatures.

The creatures did not consider beavers prey. Beavers only had to worry about some of the younger winged creatures that would attack them for no reason. They were more of a nuisance than anything.

In the past, Bronson made sure to cover his eyes from attacks by the younger creatures. *How am I going to shield my eyes and protect Clara?* Bronson contemplated. He stepped gently, hoping they would go unnoticed. Bronson knew the creatures had only one fear, so he would have to move quickly once inside the chamber.

◆ ◆ ◆

Clara saw that they were nearing the end of the tunnel. She could now see inside the chamber. It was dimly lit, like the entrance chamber they had just left. She thought the same glowing crystals were probably the source of the light.

That is odd, Clara thought, breathing heavily. *The frightful abrasive clapping sound had stopped.* She wasn't sure if that was a good thing or bad. She was so focused on the darkness of the tunnel she didn't know when the clapping sound had stopped. Now all she heard was the sound of the stream of water. *Is there a river ahead?* Clara twitched her eyes in fear. She thought back to the waterfall and how it had knocked her out of the boat into the river. "Can we go back?" Clara wanted to ask her animal friend, glancing behind her shoulder but only seeing darkness.

Clara stayed close behind the large animal that was protecting her. She was practically on his back. She gripped his shoulder, pulling his fur tightly into her hand, like a handle. Her breathing was so loud it echoed off the walls of the tunnel. The animal grunted calmly as if trying to encourage Clara as they continued down the tunnel.

Clara couldn't stop herself from thinking about the river and falling out the boat. She saw images in her mind of the violent waterfall. It was spewing water in and out of the boat, as she held onto the bench. She remembered hearing the waterfall roar with rage, "Hah hah hah, little girl!" Clara couldn't stop her thoughts. She kept thinking back to being pushed down the waterfall. The picture kept playing over and over again in her mind, tormenting her as they neared the end of the tunnel.

Sweat was pouring out of Clara's body. Her palms were wet and her fingers were slipping through the animal's fur. Her wet palms kept her from being able to hold onto its shoulder securely.

Her mind was now taking her back to the gruesome mice that attacked her and Prince Dustin in her parlor. She hoped Egon and his mouse soldiers were not in the chamber ahead.

Clara and the animal now reached the chamber.

Well, this doesn't look spooky at all, Clara thought as she let loose of the animal's shoulder. She relaxed and looked around. She thought it was quite beautiful inside the chamber. It was fairly large, not huge, but much larger than she expected. Clara glanced up and couldn't see the roof of the chamber, except in the corners, where the roof flanked down, lower than the center. The top of the chamber was black. The light didn't extend far enough up to reach that section, so Clara couldn't see how far the chamber extended up.

The walls were extremely smooth and shiny, unlike the coarse stone walls in the entrance chamber. These walls were as smooth as gemstones. Stone formations were also hanging from above, but these were massive, and like the walls of this chamber, their surface was smooth and shiny. Clara noticed the walls were the same mix of gray and white with copper and gold tones as the entrance chamber. *And I was afraid of this?* Clara thought, smiling as she looked down at all the glowing crystals on the ground.

Clara looked over to a side wall of the chamber. Water was trickling down from a small opening at a joint into a gushing stream below it. Clara thought it was nothing like the waterfall she had encountered at the river. Clara questioned if it could even be considered a waterfall.

The gushing stream of water ran through the chamber. Although the small waterfall added to the stream, the stream's main source of water was coming from someplace beyond this chamber. The gushing of the stream formed bubbles and reminded Clara of the bubble baths she used to take when she was a little girl. She'd stopped taking bubble baths a couple of years ago. Fritz still did. Mrs. Stahlbaum would fill the tub with soap, and Fritz would splash in the water, playing with his toy soldiers. Clara smiled as she thought of Fritz and his toy soldiers.

Clara's thoughts drifted and she wondered about the soldiers that had attacked the mice back in her parlor. *Where did they come from?* she wondered, rubbing her chin. *And where did they go?*

CLAP-CLAP-CLAP-CLAP-CLAP-CLAP-CLAP-CLAP-CLAP-CLAP-CLAP!

Clara jumped. The clapping noise returned. Only this time, *it was loud* and it was coming from directly above them.

CLAP-CLAP-CLAP-CLAP-CLAP-CLAP-CLAP-CLAP-CLAP-CLAP-CLAP!

Then Clara saw something fly above her! It whooshed down from the cloak of darkness at the center of the top of the chamber. Then another one, and another one, until there were so many Clara could not see through them.

"Oh no!" Clara screamed, covering her mouth in horror. She quickly looked at her animal friend. His long front teeth protruded from his lips, and his claws extended out past his paws. His fur was no longer lying flat but was sticking straight out all over his body. Her animal protector was grunting something to Clara, but it was muffled by the clapping sound.

The creatures looked like skeletal flying rats. They had long ears and wings, and no tail. They were not massive in size, not counting their wingspan, each measured less than a foot. Their faces were all exposed skin, with very little fur. Their pale shade resembled that of an albino animal.

The creatures' front teeth were long, pointed and sharp and they had a mouthful of deadly smaller teeth. They were capable of both piercing and chomping their prey. They had very long straight ears, which narrowed at the tip. Their ears accounted for one-third of their body size. The skin inside their earlobes was deeply rippled, adding to their ghastly appearance.

Clara gasped and fell back at the sight of them. Their wings scared her most of all. Their wings were jointed and translucent. When they flew, their wings flapped loudly. The winged creatures were now circling above her. Clara now knew the source of that eerie clapping sound.

❖ ❖ ❖

The clapping sound got louder and *louder* as Prince Dustin rushed through the tunnel. "Oh no!" Prince Dustin heard a scream coming from the chamber ahead. His heart started pounding even faster. He recognized the voice immediately and knew it was Clara's. He had found her, but she was in danger. He quickly wondered if the animal that took Clara was now attacking her. He hoped Egon had not found her.

CLAP-CLAP-CLAP-CLAP-CLAP-CLAP-CLAP-CLAP-CLAP-CLAP-CLAP!

The closer Prince Dustin got to the chamber, the louder the clapping sound. No, it was not Egon attacking Clara and not the animal that took her from the river, either. *The winged creatures!*

Prince Dustin was close to the entrance of the chamber. He let loose the handle of his sword, still in its sheath. He knew he would not be able to use his sword to save Clara. The cave creatures attacked as a flock, hundreds swooping down all at once. One sword would not be able to defend Clara. Prince Dustin knew he had only one chance to save her.

Prince Dustin was now at the entrance of the chamber. He saw poor Clara and the animal that had taken her. It was a beaver. He recognized the beaver at once. It was Bronson, the leader of the beaver scouts. *I should have known.* He was glad to see Bronson.

Bronson was using his body to shield Clara. Prince Dustin looked up and knew that within moments the cave creatures would be swooping down on Clara.

CLAP-CLAP-CLAP-CLAP-CLAP-CLAP-CLAP-CLAP-CLAP-CLAP-CLAP!

Prince Dustin moved quickly. He grabbed two of the glowing crystals and feverishly rubbed them together. First, white smoke started coming from the crystals. Then fire erupted.

Prince Dustin threw the fiery crystals into the gushing stream flowing through the chamber. He watched as the combustible stream burst into a continuous flame. The flame instantly engulfed the entire stream and extended up to the full height of the chamber.

CLAP-CLAP-CLAP-CLAP-CLAP-CLAP-CLAP-CLAP-CLAP-CLAP-CLAP!

The clapping sound became fast and furious as the cave creatures dispersed. They were flying as far away from the fire as they could get. Prince Dustin looked up. The cave creatures were no longer swarming above Clara and Bronson but were flying up the center of the chamber's shaft. Prince Dustin thought there must be an opening at the top of the chamber, into another part of the cave. The clapping sound got weaker and weaker until he didn't hear it at all. The cave creatures were gone.

❖ ❖ ❖

"Prince Dustin!" exclaimed Clara, running to him with wide eyes and excitement. She hugged him like she had when he was the Nutcracker Prince doll. "Those—those things, are they coming back?" Clara stuttered, still trembling as she pointed up.

Prince Dustin looked up. "They're gone."

Clara breathed a sigh of relief. "Are you okay?" she asked. Before Prince Dustin could answer, she asked question after another. "How did you know fire would scare off those, uh, whatever they were? What were they anyway? How did you find me?"

Prince Dustin chuckled as he nodded toward Bronson. "I followed his prints to the cave. I should have guessed those were Bronson's prints. And those creatures are called Nagetiere in der Nacht. They live here in the caves.

"Bronson?" Clara asked, looking over at the animal Prince Dustin called Bronson. The animal's fur was lying flat again, and his claws and teeth were no longer protruding.

Bronson grunted several times, sounding as if he was laughing. Clara raised her eyebrows in disbelief.

Prince Dustin replied, "Yes, his name is Bronson, Bronson the Beaver. He is the leader of the beaver scouts that live along the River Stromabwarts of the River Country."

"He *is* a beaver?" Clara confirmed, scanning Bronson from his head down to his toes. "I've never seen a beaver this big! Everything is so different here in the Black Forest."

Prince Dustin laughed and Bronson grunted. Clara looked at both of them and then looked down at the ground. "Can you understand him?" Clara asked Prince Dustin.

Prince Dustin felt bad. He sensed that Clara felt left out.

"Yes. Many generations back, people who live in the Black Forest made friends with some of the animals. We learned how to communicate with each other," Prince Dustin said, kicking sand up with his boots.

Bronson then started telling Prince Dustin about the meeting he had with Queen Nordika. Prince Dustin stood quite still, holding onto every word and nodding from time to time.

"Egon has assembled his best mouse soldiers, and they plan to take vengeance for the death of his brother. We must get to the Ice Palace quickly," Bronson relayed to Prince Dustin solemnly.

Clara watched Prince Dustin and Bronson. Her expression showed that she did not understand anything Bronson was communicating.

Prince Dustin then turned toward Clara and said urgently, "By going through the caves in the mountain, we will save time off our journey. Because of the cave creatures, I don't believe Egon will come through the caves. Bronson will lead us through, but we must go now!"

❖ ❖ ❖

Clara stood ready. She was glad to be leaving the caves. She looked around. The fiery stream of water was still flaming but not as strongly. She could smell a strong odor coming from the stream. She assumed that whatever the smell was, it was the cause of the water igniting.

With Bronson leading, they charged ahead into a tunnel to the left. It was on the side wall of the chamber. The tunnel was very narrow and they had to go single file. Prince Dustin made sure Clara was in the middle between him and Bronson. The farther they went down the tunnel, the darker it became until they no longer were in range of the light of the glowing crystals that lit the chamber they had left.

Clara had wanted to bring one of the crystals with them and had actually picked one up. Prince Dustin told her that Bronson could see very well in the dark. He also said that they didn't want to attract the attention of any of the other creatures that lived in the cave. Clara then dropped the crystal immediately. She didn't know what other creatures lived in the cave and didn't want to find out.

Prince Dustin and Bronson held a conversation for a while until it became pitch-black in the tunnel. Then they walked in silence. The tunnel was mostly level ground, but Clara could tell they were going downhill. She expected to be afraid, but she was not.

As they traveled through the cave, they went in and out of chambers and tunnels, stopping only for short periods of time. They collected and drank the water that seeped down from the roof from outside of the cave, it was water from the melting snow. Prince Dustin explained to Clara that the water that flowed through the cave had mineral elements, which made it combustible, so they couldn't drink it.

Clara noticed that whenever they rested, Bronson stood guard. They didn't see any cave creatures again, but from time to time, they did hear eerie sounds and clapping in the distance. In one of the chambers, Clara found a large stone rod that had become dislodged from the roof of the cave and fallen to the ground. One end of it had broken off, forming a handle-like edge, while the other end remained pointed and sharp. Clara carried it with her as they continued through the cave. She didn't know exactly what lay ahead, but she wanted to be ready. She knew it probably wouldn't be too long before they faced him—Egon.

-15-

Queen Nordika's Ice Palace

"I hope Egon and his mouse soldiers have not made it through the forest," Prince Dustin said gravely, gripping the handle of his sword.

Bronson stopped in his tracks and said something grimly to Prince Dustin.

From the short time the three of them had traveled through the cave, Clara accepted that Prince Dustin and Bronson would hold conversations without her fully understanding.

Clara didn't know what Bronson said, but both Bronson and Prince Dustin stopped walking. Prince Dustin glanced over at Clara with his cheeks flushed. Clara understood immediately that Prince Dustin was worried. It must have something to do with Egon, she thought.

"Is Queen Nordika expecting him to wage an attack at the Ice Palace or Konfetenburg?" Prince Dustin asked Bronson.

Bronson grunted.

Clara wished she could understand Bronson. She wished that she could speak with animals like Prince Dustin.

Prince Dustin then asked Bronson, with concern, "And is Drosselmeyer going to remain in Konfetenburg with Sugar Plum?"

Clara perked up when she heard Prince Dustin mention her Uncle Drosselmeyer and Princess Sugar Plum.

Bronson responded.

Prince Dustin nodded. His face was no longer tense.

Clara continued to listen and could understand bits and pieces based on Prince Dustin's comments.

"Does Egon know Drosselmeyer is in Konfetenburg?" Prince Dustin continued.

Bronson responded while raising his shoulders.

Clara didn't know the words Bronson had spoken but understood by his gesture that Bronson wasn't sure.

"Egon is vile, abominable, and quite wicked. However, he is also clever and cunning. Queen Nordika is planning for an attack," Prince Dustin said firmly to Clara.

Clara's eyes widened, "Is Egon on his way to the Ice Palace? *Is that where we are going?*"

Clara was visibly scared. Her mouth was open and her eyes welled. Prince Dustin looked at Clara. He then looked into her eyes and softly said, "I won't let him harm you, Clara."

For the remainder of their walk through the cave, all three of them remained quiet, each probably thinking about the perils ahead. For the first time since arriving in the Black Forest, Clara did not think about being home or Fritz. They heard the clapping sound in the distance, however, this time, none seemed to pay any attention. They had a bigger battle ahead of them.

◆ ◆ ◆

Clara was glad to finally be out of the cave. She glanced over at Prince Dustin and Bronson. They were both looking up ahead. Clara was still holding tight to the stone rod she'd carried from the cave. She wondered what made Prince Dustin stop and stare. His eyes twinkled as he gazed ahead. Although he always stood quite erect, his shoulders were very relaxed. Even Bronson looked calm, not standing guard.

"Clara, that's Queen Nordika's Ice Palace!" Prince Dustin exclaimed as he pointed toward the glistening palace in the distance.

Bronson grunted. He seemed to be smiling too.

Prince Dustin looked over at Clara and chuckled. "Queen Nordika is expecting us."

Clara could not speak. She stood mesmerized with her lips parted. At the top of a hill with snow-capped mountains as a backdrop, beyond the trees, almost touching the clouds, she saw a magnificent all-white stone palace.

It was totally shrouded in ice crystals making the palace look like it was made of ice. The glint from the stars above hit each crystal at such a precise angle that the crystals dazzled with prisms of color. Blues and greens and purples and gold all reflected off the crystals, forming rainbows under the night sky. From every window ledge, huge icicles of varying lengths hung in spiral shapes. Some icicles from the very top windows hung as low as two stories down. On the ground, soft, white, billowy snow glowed from the moonlight and illuminated the courtyard. The wind blew the snow ever so softly. The snow seemed to be floating and dancing, enjoying the evening.

Clara said without looking away from the palace, "That is the most beautiful place I ever saw. We don't have anything like that in my hometown. We have castles, but none look like that. It reminds me of my dollhouse." She added with a chuckle, "I was expecting it to be made of ice."

Prince Dustin smiled and said eagerly, "It is the only castle like it in the Black Forest."

The castle had one extremely wide tower that was front and center, with several taller and slimmer towers of different heights behind it. The clay roof of the towers, the only color on the castle, was deep, dark green, the same hue as the evergreen trees that were ever present in the Black Forest. Clara noticed the walls of the building held several rows of arched windows and balconies from bottom to top. A moat of ice surrounded the castle, with a wide drawbridge that connected it to the Black Forest. The drawbridge was lowered, inviting them to enter.

Clara turned when she heard Bronson. He was saying something to Prince Dustin. Prince Dustin nodded. "We must go now, Clara. Egon is not far behind."

The sight of the Ice Palace had made Clara forget about Egon and his army of mouse soldiers. Hearing Prince Dustin's comments, Clara held tight to her stone rod.

As they approached the castle, Clara noticed the courtyard was decorated with a large ornate fountain in the center. The water from the fountain had frozen solid in motion as it jetted up. Randomly placed large sculptures shaped like snowflakes, all very intricate and different, added a bit of whimsy and offset the seriousness of the fountain.

Clara's eyes moved from one sculpture to another in amazement as they walked through the courtyard. "And these are made of ice?" Clara asked, not sure if the sculptures were made of ice or crystal glass.

"Ice," Prince Dustin responded.

"Queen Nordika has probably been informed that we have arrived," Prince Dustin said.

Clara looked around. She didn't see anyone and wondered how Queen Nordika would know they were there. Clara glanced up at the windows of the tower and assumed they were being watched from above.

Clara was expecting to go directly to the front door on which hung a huge knocker, but Bronson directed them to a side door that was not locked. They were indeed expected.

They walked down a long corridor, dimly lit by sconces. Clara noticed the same glowing crystals from inside the cave were placed inside sconces that hung on the walls.

The concrete walls were white washed with stencil designs of the same ice sculptures that were in the courtyard. Falling flakes of snow were painted as a background on the walls and ceiling. Mounds of snow were painted at the bottom as if the snowflakes had drifted into piles. The tight corridor made Clara feel like she was walking through a winter wonderland. She was amazed at how real the snow looked on the walls. She wasn't surprised by how quiet the palace was, the quietness seemed to suit an Ice Palace, Clara thought. There was no sound except the sound of their footsteps on the hard concrete floor. At the end of the corridor was a big, heavy-looking arched door.

Bronson said something to Prince Dustin.

Prince Dustin turned toward Clara and said, "Queen Nordika is waiting for us in her chamber."

Clara said with excitement, her brows arched, "I've never met a queen before." She then rubbed the temple on the side of her face, and added amusingly, "I guess I've never met a prince before either."

Bronson grunted softly.

"Bronson said she is looking forward to meeting you," Prince Dustin said, walking confidently through the corridor. "She has always been an ally to my kingdom. When my parents left, Queen Nordika and your Uncle Drosselmeyer advised me and Princess Sugar Plum about our duties as Prince and Princess of Konfetenburg."

Prince Dustin continued, "She has a fierce army. Bronson said she has been preparing them to face Egon and his mouse soldiers."

❖ ❖ ❖

They made their way through the corridor and into the chamber hall. It was an extension of the corridor with white-washed stenciled walls lit by crystal sconces. However, unlike the corridor, the chamber was vibrant with sounds from the water of a marble stone fountain. The water from this fountain was flowing freely. It was not frozen like the fountain outside.

Clara smelled the scent of pine in the air. She thought she could even smell gingerbread. She knew that had to be her imagination. She was hungry. A few servants carrying silver trays walked through the chamber.

All around, playing joyfully, were all-white fluffy puppies. They were about the same size as Clara's small stuffed toy dog back at home. The puppies jumped up and down. Some were play fighting with their little jaws mouthing each other. Others were pawing each other as if playing tag.

"Look at the puppies!" Clara exclaimed.

Hearing Clara's voice, the litter of pups ran toward them and pounced up and down on Clara and Prince Dustin. None of the pups approached Bronson. Clara wasn't sure if it was because he was a beaver or the scowl on Bronson's face. Bronson grunted something as he looked down at the pups.

Yap Yap Yap Yap Yap Yap Yap Yap!

Clara bent down and rubbed the puppies. Each one vied for Clara's attention, trying to out yap the others while licking her all over. Prince Dustin chuckled as he watched little pink tongues licking Clara's face. Even Bronson seemed amused for a moment. The creaking sound of another chamber door opening distracted the pups. They scampered away. The servant that entered the chamber was now the holder of their attention.

Bronson quickly walked across the floor toward the other side of the chamber. Prince Dustin and Clara followed. Clara noticed that Prince Dustin had a little more color in his face. He was walking with the straight back of a soldier. She thought, *he must be getting stronger, getting his full strength back.*

Right when they approached a set of arched double doors, the doors opened from the other side. A large German shepherd dog stepped out. It was all white and fluffy, with a bushy tail and jet black eyes. It looked just like the pups, except it was full grown and larger. *Much larger*, Clara thought.

She stood behind the dog. She was the loveliest lady Clara had ever seen. She was very tall and slender. Dressed in all-white silk from head to toe, she stood pristinely. Her look was complete with a wreath of small white flowers she wore as a crown. Her pale white skin glistened in the light. Soft gold streaks highlighted her blonde hair. Her deep-set eyes were warm and blue, the color of the sea at the deepest part.

DEEP IN THE BLACK FOREST

With high cheekbones and a perfectly chiseled nose, if she didn't move, she would have looked like a statue, Clara thought.

The statuesque woman extended her hand and said serenely, "Hello, Clara, I am Queen Nordika."

-16-

Preparing for Battle

Clara ogled for a few seconds before gaining her composure. With her face flushed, she replied, "It is a pleasure to meet you, Queen Nordika." Clara wasn't sure if she should bow. She meekly curtsied.

Queen Nordika, as if sensing Clara's awkwardness, winked at her. Clara giggled and Prince Dustin smiled.

"Your Uncle Drosselmeyer told me all about you, Clara," Queen Nordika said in a regal manner. She tipped her head ever so slightly in Clara's direction.

"He did?"

Queen Nordika responded affirmatively with her chin held high and eyes looking directly into Clara's eyes. "Yes. He said you are a very special girl. He trusted you to take care of the Nutcracker Prince doll." Smiling, the Snow Queen added, "Which you now know was Prince Dustin."

Clara smiled back and nodded with pride as she gave Prince Dustin a quick look.

"You were very brave. If it were not for you, we don't know what might have happened," the Snow Queen added solemnly.

With her head and eyes lowered, Clara asked in a doubtful tone, *"You think I'm brave?"* Clara was glad the Snow Queen didn't know about how loudly she'd screamed when Fritz put his pet mouse in her slipper.

Queen Nordika raised Clara's head by her chin. "Yes, Clara. You are a very brave girl."

Clara looked into Queen Nordika's convincing eyes and thought *maybe*.

"It is not over yet, though, Clara. We have much left to do tonight. Egon is far more evil than his brother. I need you to continue to be brave through the rest of the night. Can you be brave against Egon?"

Prince Dustin and Bronson both looked at Clara.

Clara wasn't sure she could be brave. She wasn't even sure she had been brave. She looked at Prince Dustin. *I wasn't being brave. I was just afraid the Mouse King was going to hurt you. I was really just afraid,* Clara thought. She nodded affirmatively to Queen Nordika while avoiding looking into the Snow Queen's eyes. Clara remembered how the Mouse King kept gnawing his teeth like he was going to eat her. She wasn't sure she could be brave.

Bronson spoke with the Snow Queen and Prince Dustin. Clara was not surprised that Queen Nordika understood Bronson. The three chatted for a while. Clara understood Prince Dustin and Queen Nordika and could fill in the blanks with what Bronson was saying. Even the large white fluffy shepherd seemed attentive, Clara noticed. The shepherd wore a gold medallion dog tag and barked from time to time.

Queen Nordika informed Prince Dustin that Egon and his fiercest mouse soldiers were planning to attack Prince Dustin and Clara before he reached the Kingdom of Konfetenburg. A message was reported to Queen Nordika that Egon and his army was at the foothills and getting ready to attack the Ice Palace.

"We have less than an hour," Queen Nordika said alarmingly.

Queen Nordika's gestures and movements reminded Clara of her ballet teacher, Miss Patti. The Snow Queen was extremely graceful and her movements were precise, yet delicate. Although she was quite composed, Queen Nordika's voice was deep, throaty, and commanding, reminding all that she was the Queen of the Land of Snow.

Queen Nordika continued while walking briskly out of the chamber, "We must stop them before they reach the palace grounds!"

With that command, Prince Dustin and Bronson stiffened. They looked intensely at Queen Nordika then followed her and the shepherd out of the chamber. Clara made sure she followed closely behind them. She noticed the puppies that had been full of energy earlier were now sleeping peacefully, all curled up, on gold satin pillows beneath a large picture window. As the moon shone down on them, they looked like powder puffs.

Clara wondered what time it was. Looking at the darkness of the sky, she figured it had to be sometime in the middle of the night. For a moment, she thought about Fritz sleeping peacefully in his bed. Clara missed Fritz.

Off the chamber was another room. It reminded Clara of her parlor at home but was much larger. She noticed the walls of this room were also stenciled in snow. However, she didn't see any ice sculptures painted on the walls, just falling snowflakes. The same glowing crystals that lit the corridor and chamber were also lighting this room with a warm golden glow. In addition, a huge chandelier hung from the center of the ceiling, lighting every corner of the room.

Velvet drapes of green, with gold cords and tassels, covered arched windows, from ceiling to floor, not letting in any moonlight. A cuckoo clock hung between two large windows on the side wall, but like everything else in the Black Forest, it was also much larger than other clocks Clara had ever seen. The smell of gingerbread was even stronger in this room. A platter of gingerbread cookies on the center table caught Clara's attention. *I wasn't imagining them.*

"We must plan our attack and then I will assemble my army."

Clara glanced around the room and saw Queen Nordika speaking to Prince Dustin and Bronson. They were standing around a rectangular table in an alcove off the far corner of the parlor. The large white shepherd was also at the table. His name was General,

Clara guessed, after hearing Queen Nordika call him that several times.

"Egon sent a troop to the borders of the Land of Sweets as a guise. Drosselmeyer and your sister, Princess Leyna, were preparing for an attack there," said Queen Nordika, looking directly at Prince Dustin. Queen Nordika always referred to Princess Sugar Plum by her formal name, Princess Leyna.

"Drosselmeyer came here to warn me that Egon and his mouse soldiers planned to take revenge on you and Clara," Queen Nordika said to Prince Dustin. "Drosselmeyer explained he was going to Konfetenburg to protect your sister, Princess Leyna, from an attack. But, it was just a decoy. Egon never planned to attack the Land of Sweets."

Queen Nordika continued, "I sent an envoy to Konfetenburg to inform Princess Leyna and Drosselmeyer that Egon was not planning an attack at the Land of Sweets. That Egon actually was planning an attack here at the Ice Palace."

"The Kingdom of Mice has attacked many kingdoms in the Black Forest since my parents departed. We must stop Egon, now! If we don't stop him now, all of the kingdoms in the Black Forest will be at his mercy," Prince Dustin said strongly.

Queen Nordika and Bronson nodded.

"I must protect Clara from Egon," Prince Dustin added, looking sharply at Bronson and then over at Clara. "I knew Egon would be after Clara. I had to move quickly. I brought her here to the Black Forest to protect her from him. I will not let Egon hurt Clara."

Prince Dustin's eyes narrowed and his nostrils flared with fervor.

"I knew you would come through the Land of Snow before proceeding to Konfetenburg," said Queen Nordika. "I sent Bronson to find you so he could navigate and guide you through the tunnels in the caves, to bring you here quickly."

"I am eternally grateful to you, Queen Nordika," Prince Dustin said while bowing. "As the night continues, I am getting stronger. I expect to regain my full strength soon."

"Egon will use the strength of his army and rely on their quickness. However he is acting with rage and will make mistakes," Prince Dustin continued.

Queen Nordika acknowledged Prince Dustin with a nod.

Clara thought about how quick the mouse soldiers that attacked her in her parlor had been. Although she was afraid, she knew she could not let them harm Prince Dustin, her Nutcracker Prince.

Looking around at everyone at the table, Prince Dustin said firmly, "We will not fail!"

Clara beamed at her brave Nutcracker Prince.

While Prince Dustin and the others continued with their tactical plans, one of the Snow Queen's servants came into the parlor and placed a silver pot and cups on the center table, next to the gingerbread cookies. She signaled to Clara to help herself.

After deliberations, Queen Nordika acknowledged, "My army has been preparing since midnight and is ready for their orders."

Prince Dustin drew on a large map of the grounds that Queen Nordika had laid on the table. "The moon is bright and we will be able to see them coming. Since they don't know we are aware of their movements, we will catch them off guard."

"Where do you think I should position my army?"

Prince Dustin replied, "In the trenches around the lake that circles the front of the palace, on the other side of the drawbridge."

"Once my army is in position, I will give orders to raise the drawbridge so Egon's army won't be able to cross it," Queen Nordika said.

Prince Dustin nodded. "The soldier mice will not be able to cross the icy lake. I will attack Egon there."

Clara heard Bronson grunt and nod dutifully to Prince Dustin.

"Thank you, my dear friend, but I need you to look after Clara."

Bronson looked over at Clara and nodded with a half-bow.

Hearing her name again, Clara glanced over at Prince Dustin. She noticed the big white shepherd had gone.

The door of the cuckoo clock flung open, and the cuckoo came out spinning and chirping. While grabbing the map, Queen Nordika said, "We don't have much time. Let's get these plans to my army. Egon and his troops will be here soon."

Clara joined them. She set the stone rod she retrieved from the cave against the table. "What about me? What can I do?"

"You and Bronson will serve as lookouts. We need you in the palace tower."

Clara smiled, she was glad she was going to help Prince Dustin.

Queen Nordika then led them down a long corridor. At the end of the corridor was a staircase leading to a lower level. "My army is preparing below. They have been instructed to follow your orders. You will need this," Queen Nordika then handed Prince Dustin a black rope neckband with a small silver cylinder hanging from it.

Prince Dustin held it up in the light and then put the neckband with the silver cylinder around his neck. Clara squinted to be sure she was seeing it correctly. She wondered why Prince Dustin would need that. *It must have special powers*, Clara assumed.

At the bottom of the staircase was a large wooden door. Clara could hear the door squeak as Queen Nordika turned the lever. "My army should be ready now!"

Prince Dustin followed the Snow Queen into the lower chamber. Bronson followed behind Prince Dustin. Clara followed behind Bronson.

They all stood at the top of the lower level chamber. The room had a short ramp leading to the ground floor where Queen Nordika's army was waiting. The soldiers were all still, heads erect, ready to take their first order.

Many things about the Black Forest had surprised Clara, but none as much as this! Clara tried not to gawk but couldn't restrain herself. Her expression caught

Prince Dustin's attention. He grinned slightly as if he knew what Clara was thinking.

Prince Dustin put the small silver cylinder to his mouth and blew into it. The soldiers all stood in unison.

-17-

Battle at the Ice Palace

"Is this Queen Nordika's army?" Clara politely asked Prince Dustin, almost whispering, trying not to act surprised.

"Yes." Prince Dustin responded as he looked into Clara's wide eyes. Her right brow was arched. "The General leads her army."

Clara looked down into the cold, concrete chamber. She saw the white shepherd. General was standing at the front of the room. He was quite composed and intense with his moderately pointed ears held erect. His muscular body had smooth angles. His black piercing eyes were alert and seemed to know everything that was happening all around. His bushy tail curved. It was shaped like a saber sword. The gold medallion was still hanging around his neck. General was facing Queen Nordika's army. The soldiers occupied the entire lower chamber. They were lined up in rows.

"Well, um—I mean. Well, you know, I was expecting—" Clara was barely able to get her words out, still stunned. "*The* General?" Clara said. She nodded in the direction of the shepherd dog she thought was simply named General. Now Clara understood, the shepherd was *The General* of Queen Nordika's army.

Clara looked down into the chamber. She looked at Queen Nordika's army. The chamber was full of white German shepherd dogs. Rows upon rows of white shepherds that looked like the General, each stood with their ears erect and head forward. The shepherds were listening for their orders. They were ready for battle!

"These are my lieutenants," Queen Nordika said proudly, pointing to the shepherds in the first few rows.

Clara noticed the shepherds with the silver medallions all seemed to nod.

"And behind them are the fiercest soldiers in the Black Forest," Queen Nordika acknowledged, looking at the shepherds with blue medallions hanging from their collars.

Clara now understood why Queen Nordika had given Prince Dustin the small, silver cylinder. It was a whistle. Clara wondered what the shepherds heard when the whistle was blown, she heard only silence. With the whistle, Prince Dustin had command of Queen Nordika's army.

Hurry!" Prince Dustin said in a commanding tone. "Clara, you and Bronson will need to get to the tower."

Clara noticed that Prince Dustin's voice seemed a lot deeper than before. Something about his voice made Clara immediately jump and follow Bronson out of the chamber and back up the staircase. She knew Prince Dustin was in control.

❖ ❖ ❖

With the bright moonlight, Clara could see all of the palace grounds from the balcony of the tower. Bronson stood beside her on guard. His body did not move as if he were a mannequin. Clara noticed that Bronson's eyes were piercing and alert. They jetted from left to right, scanning the grounds and beyond.

"Bronson, Prince Dustin and the soldiers are getting in place!" Clara exclaimed while leaning against the wall of the tower.

Bronson grunted something back at her and nodded. Clara figured Bronson understood what she was saying, even though she couldn't understand him.

"Queen Nordika must be below. I heard them say she would remain in the palace and prepare for any of Egon's mouse soldiers that might make it through."

"The last troop of Queen Nordika's army is crossing over to the other side of the bridge," With the rising of the drawbridge, Clara felt the battle becoming more and more real. Clara's heart was racing and beads of perspiration formed on her forehead.

The drawbridge slowly rose up as Clara looked on desperately. She knew Egon and his soldiers were coming. Soon, her Nutcracker Prince would be face-to-face with Egon, Clara thought glumly.

Bronson looked at Clara's anxious face and grunted softly.

Clara looked at Bronson and acknowledged with a nod. Even though she didn't understand what he said, Bronson's eyes looked like they were trying to reassure her. However, Clara did not feel any more at ease.

Clara could now fully see the icy lake. The lake totally surrounded the palace grounds. She thought about how well Queen Nordika's soldiers blended in with the snow. The soldiers were almost invisible. Had the soldiers not been moving, Clara would not have seen them at all.

The soldiers rotated to the far left and right. As soon as a row was in place, they dropped down in the snow and were no longer visible. Each row of soldiers followed this same rotation on both sides of the lake.

Prince Dustin's red and blue uniform was bright against the white snow. He was walking toward a trench along the lake. "There's Prince Dustin," Clara exclaimed, "and the General." She gave Bronson a sideways glance.

Clara noticed that Bronson looked worried. His fur was again extending straight out like it had when they were about to be attacked in the cave. His eyes were glaring at something in the distance. Clara's heart beat dropped. She was momentarily frozen, paralyzed. She wanted to look in the direction of Bronson's gaze but was too afraid of what she might see.

Clara turned her head slowly. *It's Egon!* Egon and his mouse soldiers were moving between the trees in the distance. Egon was in the lead, a formidable sight to see. He moved as though he had no fear, leaving deep footprints as he trampled the snow underneath his massive body.

"Bronson, they might see Prince Dustin!" Clara shrieked.

Prince Dustin must have been aware of the approaching army of mouse soldiers too because he slid down the trench and was soon out of sight. Although Clara could still see him from the tower, she hoped that the mouse soldiers could not.

Even from a far distance, Egon made Clara shudder. She thought he looked even more vicious than his brother, the Mouse King. Egon advanced on his hind legs, wielding and slithering his smoke-gray body through the pristine white snow. Clara unconsciously stepped backward. *It's happening!*

Egon was wearing the same crown the Mouse King had worn and the red and black cape. Clara saw his hideous ringed tail, extending past his cape. It trailed behind him in the snow like a snake. Egon's soldiers randomly filed in behind him, in no apparent order. Some were walking on their hind legs, while others were on all fours. Clara shook her head and raised her hand to her mouth in fright.

"They're coming!" Clara screamed, hysterically looking left and right to both sides of the lake. Clara didn't see any of Queen Nordika's shepherd soldiers. All she saw was snow. She also could no longer see

Prince Dustin. She wasn't sure if he had changed his position or was deeper down in the trench, out of her sight.

Egon and his soldiers continued their approach. They were now in the clearing, past the trees. Bronson grunted at Clara, but again she didn't know what he was trying to tell her. Clara's head was pounding painfully, and her heart was beating faster and faster. She crouched down low on the balcony to avoid being spotted. She looked around the balcony and then gasped, "I left my rod!"

Bronson ignored her. He continued to look intensely in the direction of Egon.

Clara peeked over the balcony wall. She could now see Prince Dustin. He was still in the trenches but had moved to the center of the lake, He was near the drawbridge, closer to Egon. Clara cringed. It looked like Prince Dustin was getting ready to attack.

Egon still seemed unaware of Prince Dustin. Clara saw that Egon and his mouse soldiers kept charging forward, getting closer and closer. *"They're coming,"* Clara whispered to Bronson as she drew a frail breath. Although they were very high up, she didn't want to be overheard by Egon.

Egon stopped abruptly. He scowled as he forcefully extended his right arm straight out on his side. The mouse soldiers stopped clumsily, not in an organized fashion, but more haphazardly. The ones in the back stopped after watching the ones in front. Eventually, they all bumbled and were stationary, except for their tails. Their tails continued moving, whisking about, as if they were not controlled by the mice.

Clara cried, "They heard me!"

Bronson shook his head, indicating that they had not heard.

"What is he doing?" Clara asked in a trembling voice, as she gaped at Egon.

Bronson replied with grunts. Of course, Clara did not understand him.

❖ ❖ ❖

I have to stop him! Prince Dustin hurdled out of the trench. He wielded his sword and thrust it dead center at Egon's chest. Egon jumped back quickly, just in time to avoid being struck.

Egon was seething. Gray smoke was coming out of his nostrils. The smell of the smoke was so horrible and foul it made Prince Dustin stumble.

Egon whipped his sword in the air. He then lunged at Prince Dustin. His sword was only inches from Prince Dustin's throat. Prince Dustin staggered backward but soon regained his footing. The mouse soldiers advanced. Egon signaled them, and they stopped.

Stabbing his sword in the air and flicking it, Egon growled at Prince Dustin, "I sharpened my sword, extra sharp, just for you, Dusty!"

Egon pounced forward at Prince Dustin. Prince Dustin slid back into the snow, falling down on the ground. He quickly scooted backward to avoid being pierced by Egon's sword.

"That little girl can't save you this time. They say her name is *Clara*. Where is *Clara*, Dusty?" Egon chortled as he looked down at Prince Dustin.

Prince Dustin dug his sword into the ground and pulled his body up, as Egon laughed. He then charged forward, catching Egon off-guard. He nicked Egon deeply in his shoulder. Egon's eyes widened as if surprised by the quick assault. Although Egon did not show any signs of pain, dark red blood squirted from his body spoiling the pure white snow.

"I'm not going to let you hurt Clara!" Prince Dustin retorted fiercely.

Prince Dustin and Egon exchanged attacks. Strike followed by strike, the glint from their silver swords sparkled under the moonlight. Egon was swift, but Prince Dustin was also agile and avoided Egon's charges. The mouse soldiers watched. The battle between Prince Dustin and Egon waged on.

❖ ❖ ❖

Clara was able to see clearly from the tower. She gasped every time Egon thrust his sword toward Prince Dustin. The battle continued. To Clara, it seemed like hours passed, although it had only been minutes.

Then suddenly, Clara saw *them*. The mouse soldiers were facing the palace, watching Prince Dustin and Egon battle. They seemed to be unaware of anything happening behind them. The mouse soldiers didn't notice Queen Nordika's army of shepherds. The army of shepherds positioned themselves behind the mice at the lake.

The mouse soldiers, possibly sensing something behind them, turned around. The shock could be seen on their faces. They were now trapped by Queen Nordika's army. The invisible army of shepherds came out of hiding and was ready to battle.

The mice looked behind their shoulders at Queen Nordika's army and then turned back around and looked at the icy lake as if weighing their options. There was no escape!

Bronson grunted something to Clara. Clara thought she understood. Prince Dustin had used the fight with Egon as a distraction so that Queen Nordika's army could ambush the mice soldiers from behind.

Egon pulled back from Prince Dustin as if he realized his folly. This seemed to make Egon madder than ever. He raised his arm high in the air and thrust his sword forward. The mouse soldiers tried to charge forward but were held back by the fierce shepherds. The mice could not advance.

Queen Nordika's army was almost on top of the mouse soldiers now. The mice tried to scuttle away. Each time, they were pushed back toward the icy lake by the ferocious growls of Queen Nordika's army.

The mice spun around, slashing their tails. They tried desperately to avoid being pushed onto the icy lake. However, Queen Nordika's army kept pushing them closer and closer towards the icy lake.

Then one after another, mouse after mouse slid. The shepherds forced the mice onto the icy lake. The mice slipped and slithered. They stumbled and skidded as they fell onto the ice. Their paws and claws made it impossible for them to gain a foothold. Screams of doom erupted from the mice.

Clara chuckled. The mice became entangled into a mesh of long legs and tails. Clara was relieved to see that Queen Nordika's army had trapped the mouse soldiers on the icy lake. The ice was too slippery and the mice couldn't escape.

"Bronson, they are slipping and sliding." Clara giggled.

Bronson grunted short grunts as if he were laughing too.

Clara saw the last mouse fall onto the ice. The battle was over.

After a few moments, Clara glanced over at Bronson. His expression alarmed Clara. Bronson had stopped grunting in laughter. Bronson looked *very nervous.* His fur was sticking straight out again. Clara definitely didn't understand. *Something's wrong.*

Bronson seemed more disturbed than ever, Clara thought. He was looking down at something on the palace grounds.

"What's wrong?" Clara asked reluctantly, while slowly lowering her eyes toward the palace grounds. Then Clara saw *him.*

"It's Egon!" Clara screamed. Egon had not slid on the ice with the other mice. He had somehow escaped and was now charging through the palace grounds. Prince Dustin was following behind him, but couldn't keep up. Egon was running on all four legs, heading directly to the tower. *He must have seen me on the balcony,* Clara bemoaned.

DEEP IN THE BLACK FOREST

Bronson grunted something to Clara. He then raced down the tower steps. Clara was all alone.

-18-

Egon Attacks Clara

Prince Dustin could not catch up to Egon. *Maybe I can fly now.* Prince Dustin tried to launch himself into the air but was unable to fly. He still had not fully recovered his strength. Although he knew Bronson would protect Clara until he reached them, he was still frantic with worry.

❖ ❖ ❖

"That girl must die!" Egon cursed, speaking his thoughts as he pushed his cape behind him. "And then I will get Dusty. He will pay!" he continued, embarrassed that he'd been tricked by Prince Dustin and Queen Nordika. "I should have known the fight was a farce. Now my soldiers have been captured by Nordika's mutts!"

Egon made it to the bottom of the tower steps. He was moving so fast that had he not had on his red and black cape, he would have looked like a blur. His eyes were red hot. Smoke from his nostrils was forming tunnels behind him as he moved through the palace. He was determined to get vengeance.

Egon's rage was so intense, a blanket of doom filled the air. The little shepherd puppies that had played with Clara earlier, before falling asleep peacefully on their satin pillows, were jolted awake. They were now whining in despair as if they could feel Egon's threatening presence. The angrier Egon got, the faster he ran as he went after Clara, charging up the tower steps.

❖ ❖ ❖

Bronson knew he had to alert Queen Nordika. *Only the General can move fast enough to stop Egon from getting to the tower,* Bronson lamented. *Queen Nordika has to signal for the General.* Bronson was moving quickly through the corridors of the Ice Palace when he felt an evil, bone-chilling presence in the air. It made him stop! The fur on Bronson's coat was so straight he looked like a porcupine.

❖ ❖ ❖

I'm alone, Clara panicked.

Moments later, Clara heard something coming fast up the tower steps. She was glad that Prince Dustin was making his way up to the tower. She regretted that she had left her stone rod in the palace. She scanned the balcony, looking for something she could use as a weapon to help Prince Dustin fight Egon. She then proceeded to descend the tower stairs. *I'll meet*

Prince Dustin on the staircase and save time. He won't have to come all the way up to the tower, she reasoned

Clara was now at the top of the staircase. She then took a step to go down the stairs. The sight on the stairs made her heart stop! Clara groaned as she moved backward, away from the staircase toward the wall of the balcony. "Oh no!" Clara screamed in terror.

It's Egon! Egon looked at Clara with intense hatred. Clara cowered against the balcony wall. She looked to the left and then to the right. There was nowhere to go. *I won't be able to save Prince Dustin after all*, Clara thought tragically.

Egon moved slowly. His massive body hovered over Clara. He seemed to be deliberately teasing Clara with every step. Clara's back was pressing hard against the balcony's wall. She looked over her right shoulder. It was a long drop to the palace grounds. She dug her fingernails into the concrete wall. Although she had nowhere to go, Clara kept pressing her back against the wall, as if some magical door would open.

"You must be that little girl, Clara. Welcome to the Black Forest. Hahaha!" Clara thought she heard Egon laugh, although Clara only heard Egon snarling. She didn't really know what Egon was communicating. Whatever he was saying, it sounded so eerie that Clara cupped her ears with her hands and shook her head feverishly.

Clara was suffocating from the putrid stench coming from Egon. It smelled like Egon had been eating rotten meat. Clara thought Egon was far worse than Prince Dustin described. He was much more horrible than the Mouse King.

"Claaaaar-raaaaaa!"

Hearing Prince Dustin's voice call for Clara, Egon jerked around.

Prince Dustin stood at the threshold at the top of the staircase. At the sight of Prince Dustin, Egon went crazy. Except for his crown and cape, he was almost unrecognizable.

Prince Dustin wasted no time. With his sword held high, he pulled his elbow back and then lunged forward at Egon, thrusting his sword with great force.

Egon was quick. He averted a direct strike by jumping on top of the ledge of the tower wall. He then used the ledge to his advantage and jumped down, slamming Prince Dustin on the hard concrete floor. Prince Dustin was pinned down by Egon's hind legs and tail.

Prince Dustin pulled his arm loose from underneath Egon. With his long sword, he rammed it into Egon's tail. Egon howled loudly from the pain as he fell down. His tail was squirming back and forth, slashing against the concrete floor. Egon was hurt.

Hearing the grotesque moan, Clara cringed.

Prince Dustin wiggled himself free from underneath Egon and was back on his feet.

Egon glared up at Prince Dustin with disgust. He then pulled himself up and stood up on his hind legs. He towered over Prince Dustin. Except for Egon's red hot eyes, his face was now completely black.

Egon aimed his sword and charged recklessly toward Prince Dustin. Prince Dustin raised his sword and blocked Egon's. Egon and Prince Dustin fought back and forth even more fiercely than they had earlier. Clara panted. She felt helpless.

The crazier Egon seemed to get, the fiercer he fought. He thrashed his wounded tail at Prince Dustin as he spun around. Prince Dustin tumbled onto the concrete. Clara gasped. Egon cocked his head to the side. He then stood tall, triumphantly over Prince Dustin, with his sword at Prince Dustin's throat. With a glint of pleasure in his eye, Egon hesitated, as if he were relishing the moment.

Clara was horrified. She knew she had to save Prince Dustin, her Nutcracker Prince. She saw the blood oozing out of Egon's tail where Prince Dustin had struck him with his sword. With no time to think, Clara leaped high into the air. With all her might, she then slammed directly on Egon's tail, landing precisely on his wound. Egon bellowed in pain so loudly his scream could be heard across the palace grounds.

Prince Dustin then pulled his sword back and plunged it deep into Egon's chest. The blade went completely through Egon's body. Blood was squirting everywhere. It barely missed Clara.

Within moments, Egon passed out unconscious. Clara thought he was dead. The only sign of life coming from Egon was the slowly pumping of his body as it went up and down against the blade of Prince Dustin's sword.

Egon was no longer a threat.

❖ ❖ ❖

Queen Nordika imprisoned Egon and his mouse soldiers. All was peaceful again in the Land of Snow, as Clara and Prince Dustin stood outside the Ice Palace preparing to journey to Konfetenburg.

"Are you ready, Clara?" Prince Dustin said excitedly.

Clara responded with glee, "Yes. How long will it take to get to the Land of Sweets?"

"Not long at all."

Queen Nordika insisted that Prince Dustin and Clara take her personal sleigh. The General and a team of shepherds would take them to the Kingdom of Konfetenburg. The General was still wearing the gold medallion on his collar. The two shepherds behind him had on silver medallions. The remaining six wore blue medallions on their collars. The shepherds moved about anxiously, as much as they could while being harnessed.

Looking at the team of shepherds, Clara conveyed, "I've never ridden a sleigh before."

"You'll need to hold on tight when they turn. Queen Nordika's shepherds are very fast, and Queen Nordika told the General to get us to my castle swiftly. So they will be moving even faster tonight."

"Are you afraid, Clara?" Prince Dustin continued.

Clara responded with a smile. "Sure, I'm a little scared. Sometimes you have to do things even if you are afraid." She added, "I guess I learned that from my time here in the Black Forest." Clara then looked up. The stars were sparkling against the black velvet sky.

Prince Dustin nodded with a grin. "My sister, Princess Leyna—"

Clara interrupted him and said eagerly, "Princess Sugar Plum?"

"Yes," Prince Dustin continued with a smile. "She sent a message to Queen Nordika that the entire Kingdom is preparing for our arrival. Sugar Plum invited all the nearby kingdoms to a reception in your honor." Clara smiled humbly.

Clara turned as she heard the door of the palace open. Queen Nordika and Bronson stepped out and joined Clara and Prince Dustin.

"You are always welcome here at the Ice Palace, Clara," Queen Nordika said as she hugged Clara.

Clara, still in awe of the Snow Queen, bowed her head and meekly replied, "Thank you so much, Queen Nordika."

Bronson grunted and wrapped his broad furry arms around Clara. Although she did not know what Bronson said, she understood. "Thank you for everything, Bronson. I will miss you, too."

"Many do not know that Bronson is an ally of the Land of Snow. *Sometimes things are best kept a secret.*" Queen Nordika said to Clara. She continued, "Bronson will always be here for you too."

Clara nodded. "Thank you, Bronson."

"We have to leave, they are expecting us," Prince Dustin said softly, politely interrupting.

Clara and Prince Dustin climbed into the sleigh. The bench was soft and set back into the seat. The seats were so soft Clara thought she could fall asleep. Prince

Dustin removed his sword and placed it in a pocket behind the bench. He then blew into the small silver whistle and they were off. The moon glowed above as the sleigh slashed through the pure white snow.

The brisk air rubbed against Clara's cheeks. She marveled at the untouched snow. It was unmarred by prints of any kind. Looking above, she gazed at the tall evergreens that glistened from the snow that flocked each branch.

When they went through a heavily forested area, the tree branches blocked the moonlit sky. Clara couldn't see in front of her and wondered how the shepherds could see as they charged onward. Clara found herself holding on tightly to the side of the sleigh when they whipped around the trees. She noticed Prince Dustin's longer legs braced against the foot rest of the sleigh, preventing him from sliding around. Her legs were too short to reach it.

Clara relaxed when they reached a clearing. She thought about the battle with Egon and his mouse soldiers. "How long will Queen Nordika hold Egon and his mouse soldiers prisoners?"

"She will let the mouse soldiers go in a few days. Without Egon leading them, they won't be stirring up trouble," replied Prince Dustin.

"What about Egon?"

"He is very evil. If he were let free, he would reorganize his army and continue his attacks against the kingdoms in the Black Forest. He will remain a prisoner at the Ice Palace," Prince Dustin responded gravely.

Clara asked, "Does Egon have any other brothers?"

"No, just the Mouse King that was slain in your parlor," Prince Dustin responded.

Clara sighed in relief.

The events of the night were now rushing through her mind. She had almost forgotten about the attack by the Mouse King in her parlor. She had almost forgotten about the big Christmas party. She had almost forgotten about dancing with her little brother Fritz. She then thought about Fritz and how much she missed him.

After some time, Prince Dustin pointed toward a place in the distance. "That is my kingdom ahead."

Clara was excited to see Prince Dustin's kingdom, *The Land of Sweets*, as it was called. It was still in the far distance, but she could see a large gate with spruce and evergreen trees serving as the fence. The trees were so tall they looked as though they touched the sky.

In between the tree trunks, Clara could see a peek of the palace grounds. A large structure was in the middle. Clara assumed it was Prince Dustin's castle. While the Land of Snow and the Ice Palace reminded Clara of her dollhouses, the Land of Sweets and its castle didn't remind Clara of anything she had seen before. *This is such a wonderful place.*

Clara thought about her Uncle Drosselmeyer, whom she now understood to be a wizard. Clara remembered that Prince Dustin had said earlier that her Uncle Drosselmeyer and Princess Sugar Plum were planning for attacks at the Land of Sweets.

"Will my Uncle Drosselmeyer be here?" Clara asked.

"Yes," Prince Dustin replied.

Clara's face lit up with excitement. She had so many questions to ask her Uncle Drosselmeyer.

The shepherds slowed down. They were now approaching the gates to the Land of Sweets, the Kingdom of Konfetenburg. "Welcome to my Kingdom, Clara."

"Everywhere Clara turned she was tempted by sweets and treats, cupcakes and candy canes."

ACT 3

-19-

Land of Sweets

"Now you will see why my kingdom is referred to as the Land of Sweets, Clara," Prince Dustin said with great pride. "Princess Leyna—"

Clara interrupted, "Princess Sugar Plum."

"Yes, Princess Sugar Plum." Prince Dustin chuckled. "She has prepared a celebration for my return and to welcome and thank you for your courage."

Clara was anxious to see Prince Dustin's kingdom and meet Princess Sugar Plum. Even the General and his team of shepherds seemed to have a heightened sense of excitement. They were now prancing as they pulled the sleigh inside the castle grounds.

The courtyard was splendid and surreal. Deep, pure-white snow blanketed the grounds. Only a softly trodden pathway was clear of snow. The sound of silence was ever-present. Clara's heartbeat slowed. She felt an immediate sense of calmness and serenity taking over her. Even the General and the shepherds seemed to be relaxed and were majestically moving forward.

"Hello Clara," Clara thought she heard the trees whisper. "We welcome you to the Land of Sweets," she heard it continue. Clara glanced over at Prince Dustin. He didn't appear to have heard anything. Clara smiled.

The massive castle was the centerpiece. It was made completely of logs from the trees of the Black Forest. Covered wooden bridges connected several smaller buildings to the main structure. Although the log castle was not as tall as Queen Nordika's Ice Palace, it was far wider and amassed a much larger footprint. The castle seemed to blend in seamlessly against the backdrop of snow-capped mountains and the endless forest of evergreen and spruce flocked in snow. The trees looked like they were wearing a winter coat of white, Clara thought.

"You live here?!" Clara asked amazed. "This is like something out of one of my storybooks."

Prince Dustin replied, "Yes, this is the Log Cabin Castle. I've been told by Drosselmeyer that many stories have been written about the Black Forest. One even has a cottage made of candy. Drosselmeyer said he thought the Log Cabin Castle may have been the inspiration for some of the stories. Many were written by Jacob and Wilhelm Grimm. Have you read any of their stories?"

"I don't know. Their names sound familiar."

Prince Dustin added, "Drosselmeyer said the Grimm Brothers often journeyed to the Black Forest. Many of their stories are based on tales told to them from their travels. He said on their final journey they traveled to lands very deep in the Black Forest and barely escaped with their lives."

"Their stories must be really scary," Clara said while biting her lower lip.

"Drosselmeyer said the Brothers Grimm told him that many of the tales told from the lands in the deepest part of the Black Forest were far too scary to write. It even seemed to give Drosselmeyer shivers as he spoke of them."

"Oh my," Clara gulped.

"He said the Grimm's Fairy Tales are quite popular."

Clara looked all around. Turrets wrapped around each corner of the main building. The windows were large arch-shaped colored-glass of red, green, and gold. Light from the moon made the windows sparkle and glimmer. The windows reminded Clara of candy wrappers. She smiled at the thought.

Clara said, "This is the most wonderful place I've ever seen!"

"I'm glad you like it, Clara," replied Prince Dustin.

Prince Dustin blew into the small silver whistle. The General and his team of shepherds paraded to the left of the split pathway toward the side of the log castle. Clara saw several carriages and sleighs. She quickly assumed the horses and shepherds that drove them had been taken into a stable for the night.

From the side of the castle, Clara could see a lake. It was surrounded by several small cabins. They were also completely made of logs and had colored-glass windows that sparkled and glimmered just like the castle. They actually looked like miniature versions of the castle, Clara thought. Evergreen and spruce trees wrapped around the entire perimeter of the kingdom like a fence. There were no concrete walls or barriers.

A loud creaking sound from the opening of the side entry door caught Clara's immediate attention. A girl dressed in a pale pink satin dress with a tulle skirt came charging out.

"Dustin, you finally made it! We've all been waiting for you." Looking at Clara, the girl added, "And you must be Clara!" Without waiting for a response, the girl hugged Clara like she had known her all her life. "I am very pleased to meet you, Clara. I am Princess Leyna, but just call me Sugar Plum."

Princess Sugar Plum had reddish-brown curly hair and big, bright hazel eyes. Her eyes matched her exuberance. Her skin was a beautiful bronze tone. She was petite, slightly shorter than Clara. Sugar Plum's huge smile was contagious.

Clara was astonished that someone her own age could be so graceful. Princess Sugar Plum's delicate movements reminded Clara of Queen Nordika. Clara recalled that Prince Dustin said that Sugar Plum was a fairy, a tree fairy.

"Come, let's go inside," Sugar Plum said. "Everyone's waiting."

Prince Dustin responded as he hugged Princess Sugar Plum, "I have truly missed you, Sugar Plum."

"Is my Uncle Drosselmeyer here?" Clara asked while they entered the Log Castle.

Prince Dustin looked around. His eyes sparkled and he beamed. He was clearly happy to be home in the Land of Sweets.

"Yes, along with the entire Kingdom and nearby Kingdoms! The heads of state of each kingdom brought entertainment and food delicacies for the celebration," Sugar Plum said ecstatically.

Clara looked up at the starry sky. She didn't know what time it was, but it was not yet morning. Clara was surprised they would be holding a celebration at this hour of the night. *Life is very different deep in the Black Forest*, Clara acknowledged silently.

As they walked into the corridor of the castle, Clara could smell sweets of all kinds. Her stomach growled. Clara patted her belly, hoping no one heard it rumble.

Prince Dustin's castle was rustic but grand...very grand in a rustic kind of way. Instead of paintings—images of bears, wolves, and other animals were carved into the wooden walls. Clara saw candy and cookies. Pastries, puffs, and pies were everywhere. All kinds of goodies were on platters, in bowls, and under covered dishes. Everywhere Clara turned she was tempted by sweets and treats, cupcakes and candy canes. Gumdrops of every color were overflowing out of their dishes, while gingerbread men with white icing faces were stacked neatly on plates.

Prince Dustin saw Clara ogling at the candy and said, "You can help yourself to anything, Clara."

"Thank you," Clara said, as she picked up a chocolate-covered bon-bon with a swirl of vanilla icing. "Mmmmm," she cooed softly as she bit into soft, sweet, creamy caramel.

The closer they approached the Great Hall, the noisier it got. Clara could hear the sound of all sorts of musical instruments. She recognized the sound of a piano and violin and trumpets and drums. The sounds were overlapping as though several separate groups of musicians were rehearsing at the same time. She also heard the pattering of feet, some stomping, and some lightly tapping. The sound reminded Clara of her dance school.

"Your Uncle Drosselmeyer wants to speak with you before the celebration begins. He is waiting for you in the library," Sugar Plum told Clara. "And, Dustin, you will have just enough time to change your clothes." Looking at Prince Dustin's stained uniform, she added, "I was so worried about you and am glad you defeated Egon. After you've changed, will you meet Clara in the library and bring her to the Great Hall?"

Prince Dustin nodded.

Clara stepped inside the library. Sugar Plum closed the door behind Clara.

Clara did not see her Uncle Drosselmeyer in the library, at first. The room was filled from floor to ceiling with bookcases full of books. A grand fireplace with a roaring fire was on the side wall warming the room.

DEEP IN THE BLACK FOREST

A great-grandfather clock was on the opposite wall. The time on the clock was slightly after midnight. Clara assumed the clock was broken. Two large leather chairs faced a large desk. The desk was made of the same dark wood as the bookcases.

A nutcracker doll on the desk caught Clara's attention. *It looks just like my Nutcracker Prince doll!* Clara said softly. She rushed over to the desk to examine the doll up close.

"Clara!" Clara heard the pleasant voice of her Uncle Drosselmeyer.

Clara turned around and suddenly saw him. Her Uncle Drosselmeyer was standing by the great-grandfather clock. She hadn't heard him come into the room. She wondered if she had possibly just missed seeing him. Then she thought, of course, he's a wizard.

Next to her Uncle Drosselmeyer, Clara saw Helmut.

Clara ran to her Uncle Drosselmeyer and gave him a big hug, "Uncle Drosselmeyer!" She then bent down and rubbed Helmut, "Hi Helmut!"

"Dear Clara, I know you've had a very adventurous evening!"

Clara could no longer hold anything in. The events of the night came spilling out. She shared with her Uncle Drosselmeyer how her Nutcracker Prince doll had come to life. Then she acknowledged, "Well, you already know about that."

She told Drosselmeyer about the Mouse King and how the Nutcracker Prince slew him. She talked about flying with Prince Dustin from her parlor to the Black

Forest. She told him about Queen Nordika and the Ice Palace.

She continued and told him how she had been afraid. She recounted how she jumped high in the air, like the teenage dancers in her ballet school, and stomped on Egon's wounded tail. She spoke so fast she was able to recount the entire evening in a matter of minutes.

"I'm so proud of you, Clara. I knew you would protect the Nutcracker Prince doll. I knew you would overcome your fears." Herr Drosselmeyer beamed with pride as he looked at Clara. Hel4mut barked, seemingly in agreement.

The door to the library opened. Prince Dustin stepped in, "Are you ready to go to the celebration, Clara?"

Clara turned and looked at Prince Dustin. "Yes, I just wanted to ask my Uncle Drosselmeyer—" Clara turned back around toward her Uncle Drosselmeyer. However, Drosselmeyer and Helmut were both gone! They disappeared. Clara glanced over at the desk. The Nutcracker Prince doll was gone, too.

Clara was flushed. She turned back toward Prince Dustin. "Yes, I guess I'm ready." She hadn't gotten to ask her Uncle Drosselmeyer about getting back home.

"They are ready to begin the celebration!" Prince Dustin exclaimed, interrupting Clara's thoughts.

Clara was looking forward to the celebration. The music was now louder than ever. She looked out the corner of her eye at Prince Dustin. She was happy she distracted the Mouse King and Egon. She was happy that she had been brave.

Clara beamed radiantly as she and Prince Dustin entered the Great Hall.

-20-

The Celebration

"Honored guests, I would like to welcome home my brother, Prince Dustin Egbert Conrad von Konig." The guests all clapped. "I would also like to introduce you to Clara!" exclaimed Princess Sugar Plum. "We are very thankful to Clara for her bravery and courage against the Mouse King and his evil brother Egon."

Princess Sugar Plum curtsied and all in the room followed. The ladies and girls curtsied and the men and boys bowed. The room went silent. Not a sound could be heard, no clanking of glasses, no movement of feet, complete silence.

As Clara and Prince Dustin stood just inside the doorway of the Great Hall, Clara immediately understood why it was called the Great Hall. It was enormous. It was bustling with dignitaries and guests from all across the nearby kingdoms. Clara's eyes couldn't span the room fast enough. There was so much to see. Princess Sugar Plum was speaking, but Clara was so entranced, she didn't hear a word.

The people of each kingdom all dressed similarly, but very differently from the people of the other kingdoms. Fabric and garb in vibrant colors of orange and red to blue and gold could be seen everywhere. Clara looked at Prince Dustin. He had changed into a new uniform, still red and blue, but this one was adorned with gold bands and copper buttons.

Clara looked down at her own clothes. She was still wearing her gown and pantaloons. She would have normally felt out of place, but the faces and smiles of everyone in the room put her immediately at ease.

After the brief pause, the music started back up ceremoniously. Clara heard the smooth sound of a harp as it blended harmoniously with horns, flutes, and other instruments that she recognized from her ballet classes.

"May I have the honor of a dance, Clara?" Prince Dustin politely asked while bowing.

Clara responded with a graceful curtsy. She then took Prince Dustin's arm as he escorted her to the center of the dance floor.

Clara and Prince Dustin danced the waltz in perfect unison, moving as one across the dance floor. She held her head erect, shoulders high with her back straight and tilted slightly backward on an angle. She danced just like she did in dance class.

Clara avoided looking into Prince Dustin's eyes. She danced in her space as they swayed and turned. They glided smoothly all across the floor. The room erupted into oohs and ahhs as Clara and Prince Dustin spun and twirled. Clara wondered how Prince Dustin learned how to dance. The room burst into thunderous applause when they concluded their waltz. Prince Dustin raised Clara's hand in salute. Clara responded with a modest curtsy.

Princess Sugar Plum walked ever so gracefully across the floor. She was so graceful that even when she walked, she looked like she was gliding. A hush took over the room. All eyes watched every step as Princess Sugar Plum captivated everyone in the Great Hall.

"Clara, these flowers are for you as a small token of our appreciation for your bravery," Princess Sugar Plum announced as she presented Clara with a bouquet of flowers.

"Thank you, Princess Leyna." Clara then quickly corrected herself, "I mean Princess Sugar Plum." Calling Sugar Plum by her formal name, Princess Leyna, just came out naturally. She commanded the room with such grace and elegance befitting of the name Princess Leyna.

Princess Sugar Plum was like the princesses Clara read about in her storybooks, poised and elegant. Although regal, Sugar Plum was very enchanting all the same, Clara observed.

"All the kingdoms are here to entertain you and Prince Dustin with music and dance!"

"Clara," Prince Dustin said pointing across the room. "Those are our seats for the festivities," Prince Dustin added. He then escorted Clara to elaborately embellished red velvet high-back chairs. The chairs were set on a platform so they could easily view the entertainment. The celebration had officially begun.

Prince Dustin and Clara had hardly had a chance to take their seats when the fast beat of dancers from the Kingdom of Schokolade took to the floor. A male and female dancer, dressed in red velvet with black lace, was set to perform. The dancers chassed and turned as they gyrated across the floor. The female dancer held an elaborate fan. At times, she hid her face coyly from her male partner.

Prince Dustin informed Clara, as he nodded toward the dancers, "They are from the Land of Chocolate."

"I wish my dance teacher, Miss Patti, could see them dance!" Clara exclaimed, without her eyes leaving the dancers.

Clara was so enthralled with the fast movements and precise arm gestures that she found herself imitating the dancers while seated. She raised her arms in the same sharp, jerky style as the dancers.

"Her head almost touched the floor!" Clara exclaimed. She noticed how flexible the female dancer was as the dancer fully extended her back into a backward arch, almost touching the floor.

As soon as the dancers from the Land of Chocolate stepped off the floor, the next group of dancers quickly moved into place at the center of the dance floor.

They represented the Kingdom of Kaffee. Clara relaxed in her seat as she watched the sultry dancers move to the mysterious sounds of the clarinet and flute. The dancers began with the female dancer being balanced in the air, in a seated position by her male partner.

The female dancer held her arms above her head in a diamond shape with her palms touching. She softly moved her head from left to right between her arms. As the male dancer slowly brought his female partner to the floor, she slowly moved to form various contortions with her body. She danced gracefully using her arms and hands as much as her legs and feet. Her dancing started at her shoulders and continued through her fingertips.

Clara was in total awe when the female dancer raised her leg behind her and grabbed her foot with both hands. The dancer gracefully let go and began to nose dive to the floor. The dancer's forehead touched the calf of her leg. The dancer then quickly formed a full side-split with her left leg held at her ear.

Clara was at the edge of her seat. She exhaled at the end of their performance as if she were the one dancing.

Clara exclaimed as if exhausted, "I've never seen any dancing like that before. They remind me of a pretzel the way they twisted their bodies."

Prince Dustin smiled and nodded as a servant brought over a silver tray with a variety of sliced meats and cheeses, fruits and vegetables, along with a bevy of sweets. "Clara, would you like something to eat?"

"Thank you," Clara responded while taking a small plate off the tray and filling it with a little of everything. "Those dancers were the best I've ever seen. I don't know how she could raise her legs so high! I think I would have split in half." Clara chuckled animated.

Prince Dustin replied, "You are a great dancer, too, Clara. Did you learn to waltz in your dance class?"

"Yes. Miss Patti taught us how to waltz. Fritz had to learn to dance the waltz, too. My mother taught him, though. He doesn't like it, but my mother makes him practice with me at home."

A group of three male dancers got Clara's attention. They donned red boots and were jumping wildly. They kicked their heels and jumped into full splits in the air. They shouted and clapped while they danced.

The dancers looked fierce as they jumped high, full of excitement and powerful moves. Clara was amazed by their fancy footwork and couldn't understand how they could dance in boots. "Can you dance like that?" she asked Prince Dustin.

Prince Dustin gulped, without responding.

Clara and Prince Dustin continued to chat and eat while other dancers performed. Clara applauded robustly after each group. She recognized many of the dance moves. However, she had never seen dancers move so effortlessly with such exact precision. She watched intently, trying to learn some of their dance techniques.

Although the music hadn't started playing, the Great Hall was suddenly quite noisy as the next group moved into position. A very, very tall, matronly lady, with an extra-large satin skirt in a patchwork of vibrant colors, slowly made her way to the center of the dance floor.

Clara looked curiously at the matronly lady. She heard a cackling of children's voices echoing off the walls of the Great Hall. Clara looked around the room. She thought it odd that she didn't see the children that were making all the noise. The children's voices seemed to be coming from underneath the matronly lady's skirt. Clara looked confused at the lady's skirt.

The music started the moment the matronly lady positioned herself at the center of the dance floor. Then—one by one—they jumped! They jumped out from underneath the lady's skirt! A boy jumped out first... then a girl. Boys and girls continued jumping out from underneath the skirt. The crowd erupted into laughter.

The lady's skirt was a curtain. Clara glared underneath the lady's skirt. She noticed the lady was actually walking on wide boards that made her appear tall. Clara looked closely at the matronly lady's funny face and laughed uncontrollably. The matronly lady had a beard and mustache.

"Do you see the stilts?" Prince Dustin laughed as he pointed to the wide boards.

Clara, still laughing, nodded.

The children were dressed gaily in vibrant satin of blues and gold, greens and violet. Clara couldn't move her eyes fast enough from dancer to dancer. Some were doing somersaults across the dance floor, first going forward, then backward. Others were partnered and danced the polka.

They were so much fun to watch, that Clara wanted to join them on the dance floor. Before she knew it, the children were throwing kisses to the audience as they made their way back underneath the skirt.

The matronly-looking performer, Mother Ginger, Clara heard someone call her, waved at Clara before turning around to exit the dance floor.

The room got darker and darker. Then became quiet, there was not a sound.

Clara thought the festivities were over. Then she noticed that everyone was looking toward the far corner of the room. Clara looked in the same direction.

Then Clara saw her! The girl dancer moved slowly as she stepped gently. A crystal spotlight followed her as she moved. Her feet seemed to barely touch the floor. Clara wasn't sure if the dancer was walking or floating in the air.

"That's Princess Sugar Plum?!" Clara screamed as she shot a questioning glance at Prince Dustin. Clara already knew the answer.

Clara could tell a great dancer. Many dancers from faraway places came to her dance studio to rehearse for performances. They all walked with perfect posture with their necks elongated. Although graceful and elegant, they all walked with their feet slightly turned outward. *Like a duck*, Clara thought.

Princess Sugar Plum had on the same pink dress with tulle skirt. Her hair was now pulled high on top of her head in a perfect bun. On top of her head, she wore a crown of crystals and pink gemstones that sparkled when the crystal spotlight reflected off them. Every eye in the room was on Princess Sugar Plum. Prince Dustin told Clara that Tree Fairies were known to be extraordinary dancers.

"I should have guessed she was a dancer," Clara said.

The music began softly as Princess Sugar Plum stepped to the center of the room. The music sounded like water drops from a fountain. Clara listened closely as she watched.

Princess Sugar Plum began dancing. She danced gracefully and slowly. She moved so slowly, at first, that no one was aware when the dance actually began. She elegantly and gently extended her arms out to both sides.

Princess Sugar Plum flicked her fingertips, as though they were musical instruments. The soft arch of her foot then became her musical instrument. She gently tapped her toe to the floor in a semi-circle, matching the beat of the music. She then slowly began turning. She followed pirouette after pirouette after pirouette, flicking her leg backward at every turn.

All in the room were silent. Princess Sugar Plum swirled and fluttered her feet while moving backward. She reminded Clara of a butterfly fluttering from flower petal to flower petal. Princess Sugar Plum continued dancing to the delight of everyone in the Great Hall.

Princess Sugar Plum then spun and spun and spun. She gracefully twirled all around the room. She seemed to be magically moving backward while turning. Clara got dizzy watching. Fouetté after fouetté after fouetté, Sugar Plum danced.

Then dramatically, Princess Sugar Plum stopped in a strong fourth position. The room exploded into pandemonium. Princess Sugar Plum bowed deeply several times, extending her right arm out to her side. She then, ever so gracefully, walked back to the far corner of the room where she'd begun.

Everything happened so quickly at that point. Clara found herself getting sleepy and tried hard to keep her eyes open. Prince Dustin watched as all the dancers who had performed rushed to the center of the floor, dancing. All the guests joined in and soon everyone was dancing. Prince Dustin looked over at Clara. Clara was sound asleep. Prince Dustin lifted Clara off the red velvet chair. Princess Sugar Plum was now beside him.

"Clara has had a very long night," Princess Sugar Plum said to Prince Dustin.

Prince Dustin smiled and replied, "This was a very long night, indeed."

"I will go with you to take her to her bed," Princess Sugar Plum said. Prince Dustin nodded.

-21-

Christmas Day

"Clara! Clara! Wake up!" shouted Fritz as he jumped up and down on Clara's bed.

Clara shifted and pulled her blanket over her head to shut out the noise that was trying to wake her. She'd dreamt about a handsome prince in a faraway land and an Ice Palace with a beautiful queen dressed all in white.

There were dogs and puppies and beavers in this strange land. All the animals could talk with people. She was dreaming of eating chocolate bonbons and gingerbread cookies while dancers were jumping and spinning and pirouetting. She had a vision of an amazing dancer called Sugar Plum, who was actually a fairy.

The dream took her on a journey deep in the Black Forest. There was a battle with mice, not regular mice like Fritz's pet mouse. These were large scary creatures, larger than Clara. One was extremely frightful. It had red eyes and smoke came out of its nostrils. Clara shuddered and tossed in her bed as she thought about that mouse.

Her Uncle Drosselmeyer had even been in the dream. He was a wizard. He had turned a handsome prince into a Nutcracker Prince doll, and then back into a prince. She'd dreamt about wanting to ask her Uncle Drosselmeyer a question. She couldn't remember the question.

"Clara! Wake up. It's Christmas morning," Fritz said, even louder than before, as he tugged the blanket off Clara.

Clara rubbed her eyes and yawned. She then stretched her arms above her head. She was slowly waking up. She opened her eyes, expecting to see Prince Dustin and Princess Sugar Plum. Clara looked around intensely, "Where is Prince Dustin?"

"Who?" said Fritz confused. He shook Clara. "Come on, Clara, wake up!"

Just then, Fritz's pet mouse fell out of the breast pocket of his pajama top onto Clara's lap. The little white mouse sat there looking directly into Clara's eyes. Fritz raised his hand and was about to grab the little mouse. He saw the smile on Clara's face and pulled his hand back.

Clara picked up the little white fluffy mouse while resting her back against the headboard of her bed. Fritz watched anxiously with a curious look on his face.

With the mouse cupped in her hand, Clara raised the mouse to her eye level and said, "Good morning, little mouse." Clara stroked the mouse gently down its back with her index finger.

Fritz responded with skepticism, "Clara, you aren't afraid of my mouse?"

Clara had to think about that question for a moment. The last time she'd seen Fritz's little white mouse, it was jumping out of her slipper when she was getting dressed for the Christmas Eve party. She suddenly sat up straight while wildly looking around her room. She handed the little mouse back to Fritz and asked rather loudly, "How did I get back home?"

Fritz looked at Clara strangely, as if he wanted to ask what she meant. Clara rattled off a series of questions as she jumped out of bed and ran to her bedroom window. She looked out the window anxiously as if she was looking for something.

Clara said with desperation, *How did I get here? Where is Prince Dustin?!*"

This was the second time Clara had asked about Prince Dustin. "Are you okay, Clara?" Fritz asked concerned.

Clara turned around anxiously. She looked around her bedroom and then at Fritz. She stuttered, "Y-y-yes, I'm okay, Fritz. I guess—I guess I was just dreaming."

Fritz sighed with relief, as he eagerly grabbed Clara's hand and pulled her arm. "Come on. Mom and Dad are downstairs. It's time to open our Christmas presents."

Clara smiled as she let Fritz lead her downstairs. She was half running to keep up. Clara stopped at the top of the staircase. She listened for the screeching-scratching-skittering she had heard in her dream, the sound that had led her downstairs in the middle of the night. Fritz jerked Clara's hand motioning her to continue, before letting her hand go.

"Come on!" he shouted. Then Fritz raced down the stairs.

Clara followed quickly behind Fritz. She smelled the hickory scent of sausage and baked apples and cinnamon as she galloped down the stairs. She could hardly wait to eat the marzipan streusel cake and marmalade that Mrs. Koch made every Christmas morning. Clara also thought about the roasted goose Mrs. Koch prepared every Christmas for dinner.

Fritz was already kneeling underneath the Christmas tree with a wrapped present. He yanked at the ribbon and was tearing the paper wrapping by the time Clara made it to the parlor. Clara quickly noticed that everything looked to be in its proper place, not ransacked from the battle with the Mouse King. Clara thought, *yes it was just a dream.*

"Merry Christmas, Clara," Mrs. Stahlbaum said as she gave Clara a big hug.

Dr. Stahlbaum was standing over Fritz, looking as eager as Fritz. Dr. Stahlbaum briefly looked over his shoulder at Clara. "Merry Christmas, Clara. Did you sleep well?" He didn't look at her long enough to make Clara think he really wanted an answer. Clara smiled, not knowing how to answer her father's question.

Dr. Stahlbaum and Fritz always seemed the most excited about opening presents. Every Christmas, Dr. Stahlbaum, and Fritz played all morning with the new toys Fritz got on Christmas day.

Clara's mother smiled and repeated, "Did you sleep well, Clara? I thought I heard you get up in the middle of the night."

As soon as Mrs. Stahlbaum completed her sentence, Clara blurted out with exasperation, "Mom, you heard me get up last night?" She thought maybe it wasn't a dream after all. She then told the adventure she had deep in the Black Forest starting with the mice chasing her. "The Nutcracker Prince doll turned into a real prince, Prince Dustin."

Mrs. Stahlbaum said, "Oh my." Clara didn't think her mother believed the story.

By now, Dr. Stahlbaum had joined Fritz on the floor. They were building a castle from a kit for Fritz's toy soldiers. Mrs. Stahlbaum took a seat on the sofa as she listened to Clara.

Fritz quickly looked at Clara and said, "Not that Prince Dustin story again?"

Clara exclaimed, "And there were castles, too!" trying to gain support from Fritz and her father. "One was called the Ice Palace, but it wasn't really made of ice."

Fritz replied, "Then why was it called the Ice Palace?"

Clara, frustrated replied, "Because it was in the Land of Snow. Queen Nordika even had dogs that she called shepherds. The shepherds were her army. They fought off Egon's army of mouse soldiers."

"The dogs were fighting little mice?" Fritz chuckled.

"No! They were not little. They were as large as Father. Last night Prince Dustin slew the Mouse King, right where you are sitting now, Fritz!" Clara exclaimed.

Laughing, Mrs. Stahlbaum asked Mrs. Koch, who had stepped into the room, "Did someone accidentally put champagne in the children's punch?"

Mrs. Koch, taking Mrs. Stahlbaum seriously, shook her head several times. "No, Mrs. Stahlbaum."

Mrs. Koch looked puzzled as she checked the corners of the room.

Ding-Dong! Ding-Dong! Ding-Dong!

Mrs. Koch turned to answer the door. A smile again returned to her face.

Clara shrugged and hung her head, "Nobody believes me."

"Merry Christmas, Mrs. Koch. How are you doing this fine Christmas morning?"

Clara heard the sound of her Uncle Drosselmeyer's voice. She jumped up from the chair she had crouched down in and darted to the front door.

Clara ran to her Uncle Drosselmeyer. Before he could give her a hug, Clara grabbed his hand and pulled him into the parlor. Mrs. Koch followed them, moving quickly.

"Tell them, Uncle Drosselmeyer," Clara said loudly, with vindication, as she looked up at her Uncle Drosselmeyer.

Everyone was now looking at Drosselmeyer, waiting for his response. Mrs. Koch was now sitting beside Mrs. Stahlbaum on the sofa, on the edge of her seat. She stared straight into Drosselmeyer's mouth.

Mr. Godfrey entered the parlor. He could barely get out, "Merry Christma—" before Mrs. Koch shushed him to be quiet. Everyone was now looking at Clara and Drosselmeyer as they stood in the center of the parlor.

Clara continued, "Tell them, Uncle Drosselmeyer. That you were there last night. That Prince Dustin did fight off the Mouse King and took me with him deep in the Black Forest."

"Tell them that people can talk with animals and how the beaver Bronson protected me from the winged creatures in the cave. Oh yes, I almost forgot about them," Clara said, interrupting herself.

"Tell them how Prince Dustin fought off Egon. Tell them how Princess Sugar Plum invited all the people of the nearby kingdoms to the celebration at Prince Dustin's castle in the Land of Sweets."

"She gave me flowers for being brave. Tell them you are really a wizard. Tell them, Uncle Drosselmeyer!" Clara was now looking at everyone. She was standing tall and victorious, with her hands on her hips. *They will have to believe me now*, she thought.

Clara waited anxiously. Not hearing anything from her Uncle Drosselmeyer, she looked up at him for support.

Herr Drosselmeyer responded as he winked to everyone else, "Sure, Clara."

Immediately everyone in the parlor let out a roaring laugh, even Mrs. Koch, and Mr. Godfrey. Clara lowered her head. Nobody believed her.

Then suddenly she remembered the Nutcracker Prince doll. "Remember, Uncle Drosselmeyer? You turned the Nutcracker Prince doll back into a prince, Prince Dustin," Clara said, trying to get her Uncle Drosselmeyer to remember.

"I left the Nutcracker Prince doll underneath the Christmas tree last night. When the Mouse King and soldier mice came, you turned the doll into a prince, *a real prince*, Prince Dustin. Remember?"

The room was now completely quiet. All eyes slowly turned to the Christmas tree. Everyone looked down at the little toy bed where Clara had placed the Nutcracker Prince doll before she went to bed.

They looked past Fritz and Dr. Stahlbaum. They both had stopped playing. Everybody was looking underneath the tree. They then spotted the little toy bed—.

Clara gasped. The Nutcracker Prince doll was safely tucked in the little toy bed.

With sympathetic-looking eyes, Mrs. Stahlbaum quickly announced, "It's time for breakfast. Everyone, please join me in the dining room." She then gave Clara a big hug and said, "Dreams can sometimes seem very real, Clara. You had a vivid dream indeed."

Everyone followed Mrs. Stahlbaum into the dining room. Mrs. Koch jumped up first and rushed ahead of everyone.

Clara watched everyone leave the parlor. Drosselmeyer was the last to leave. "Clara, come to breakfast. *You should be very tired and hungry.*" He then turned and followed everyone into the dining room. She was frustrated that nobody believed her story. *She even no longer believed her story.*

Clara walked over to the Christmas tree and picked up her Nutcracker Prince doll. She looked up at the ceiling in the parlor. Holding the doll, she stepped behind the Christmas tree. She looked out the window, the same window where she'd dreamt that she and Prince Dustin stood before they flew to the lands deep in the Black Forest.

Clara thought about her dream. Even though it was a dream, she would never forget Prince Dustin. She then looked down at her Nutcracker Prince doll. As she looked down, she saw something glowing underneath her gown!

She pulled out the crystal necklace Prince Dustin had given her to keep her warm deep in the Black Forest.

It wasn't a dream!

Clara smiled as she held the crystal necklace. After a few minutes, she tucked the crystal necklace back underneath her gown. She then tightly hugged her Nutcracker Prince doll. She remembered what the Snow Queen had said to her before she and Prince Dustin departed for the Land of Sweets, "*Sometimes things are best kept a secret.*"

Clara then joined everyone in the dining room for Christmas breakfast.

–The End

Resources & Notes

The Nutcracker ballet has been enjoyed by audiences around the world, ever since its premiere in St. Petersburgh, Russia in 1892. The ballet was based on the re-telling of E. T. A. Hoffmann's story, *The Nutcracker and the Mouse King,* by **Alexandre Dumas** in his adaptation, *The Tale of the Nutcracker.* The setting of *The Nutcracker* ballet is Germany in the 19th century. The ballet was originally choreographed by Marius Petipa and Lev Ivanov with a score by Pyotr Ilyich Tchaikovsky.

E.T.A. Hoffmann was named, Ernst Theodor Wilhelm Hoffmann, at birth. Later, he changed Wilhelm to Amadeus after Mozart. In **Prince Dustin and Clara: Deep in the Black Forest,** Clara's father is named Wilhelm. Almost all the characters in the book have actual German names that depict their character's personality. One exception is Clara's dance teacher, **Miss Patti.** That name was chosen as an homage to Daniel Lee Nicholson's first ballet instructor in Chicago. Daniel performed in various productions of *The Nutcracker* ballet spanning over 10 years. Nicholson noted that when writing the story, *Prince Dustin and Clara: Deep in the Black Forest,* the language setting often switched to German because of the author's use of German terms and words.

The **Black Forest** was chosen as the setting for the Snow Scene in *Prince Dustin and Clara: Deep in the Black Forest,* because of its proximity to the original setting of the ballet. It is also believed that **Wilhelm and Jacob Grimm** were inspired by the Black Forest when they published many of their *Grimm's Fairy Tales.* The Black Forest is full of enchantment and history. The author, Nicholson, ensured to include some of the allure of the Black Forest in the book.

We at Fossil Mountain Publishing hope you have enjoyed our re-telling of the classic fairy tale and will tell your family and friends about the book. Although the book can be enjoyed year-round, we encourage you to enjoy an actual performance of *The Nutcracker* ballet during the holiday season.

Additional resources and information can be found on the following websites:

www.FossilMountainPublishing.com

www.PrinceDustinAndClara.com

About Us

Author

Daniel Lee Nicholson was born and raised in the Midwest. He has been a performer and ambassador of the performing and fine arts ever since his first performance as a soldier in *The Nutcracker* in Chicago. He resides with his wife in the Los Angeles area and works in the Media and Entertainment industry. *Deep in the Black Forest*, is his debut novel in the series: **Prince Dustin and Clara.**

Publisher

The mission of Fossil Mountain Publishing LLC (www.FossilMountainPublishing.com)
is to captivate and entertain; engage and inspire young readers and readers of all ages by publishing family-oriented books that promote reading and literature; technology and the arts. We strive to develop applications and to incorporate technology into our platforms so that our readers can fully immerse themselves in great stories.

❖ ❖ ❖

Cover-Artist

Luke Ahearn (www.LukeAhearn.com) is a lifelong artist born in New Orleans, LA that now lives in Central California. He is a successfully published author of both fiction and nonfiction. Many of his books are in their 2nd, 3rd, and 4th editions. His art has been most recently featured on HGTV, Pool Kings. In addition to the cover, the interior artwork was also created by Luke.

CPSIA information can be obtained
at www.ICGtesting.com
Printed in the USA
LVOW12*0132180518

577643LV00002B/9/P